First World War
and Army of Occupation
War Diary
France, Belgium and Germany

25 DIVISION
Divisional Troops
113 Brigade Royal Field Artillery
25 September 1915 - 28 February 1917

WO95/2234/2

The Naval & Military Press Ltd
www.nmarchive.com
Published in association with The National Archives

Published by

The Naval & Military Press Ltd

Unit 10 Ridgewood Industrial Park,

Uckfield, East Sussex,

TN22 5QE England

Tel: +44 (0) 1825 749494

www.naval-military-press.com

www.nmarchive.com

This diary has been reprinted in facsimile from the original. Any imperfections are inevitably reproduced and the quality may fall short of modern type and cartographic standards.

© Crown Copyright
Images reproduced by permission of The National Archives, London, England, 2015.

Contents

Document type	Place/Title	Date From	Date To
Heading	WO95/2234/2 113 Brigade Royal Field Artillery		
Heading	113th. Brigade R.F.A. Sep 1915-Feb 1917		
Heading	25th Division 113th Bde. R.F.A. Vol I Sept. & Oct. 15. Feb. 17		
War Diary	Aldershot	25/09/1915	25/09/1915
War Diary	Southampton	25/09/1915	25/09/1915
War Diary	Havre	26/09/1915	26/09/1915
War Diary	Havre Caestre	27/09/1915	28/09/1915
War Diary	Caestre	29/09/1915	29/09/1915
War Diary	Oosthove Camer	30/09/1915	13/10/1915
War Diary	Oosthove Fm	14/10/1915	29/10/1915
Heading	25th Division Nov. 15. 113th Bde. R.F.A. Vol 2		
War Diary	Oosthove	01/11/1915	29/11/1915
Heading	25th Divs. 113th Bde. R.F.A. Vol. 3		
War Diary	Oosthove Nieppe B 11 C. 10.4	01/12/1915	30/12/1915
Heading	113th. Brigade R.F.A. 25th. Divisional Artillery January 1916.		
War Diary	Oosthove Nieppe B 11 C. 10.4	01/01/1916	25/01/1916
War Diary	Eecke	31/01/1916	31/01/1916
Miscellaneous	Appendix I	24/01/1916	24/01/1916
Heading	113th. Brigade R.F.A. 25th. Divisional Artillery February 1916		
War Diary	Eecke	01/02/1916	03/02/1916
War Diary	Volkerinckhove	04/02/1916	12/02/1916
War Diary	Eecke	14/02/1916	18/02/1916
War Diary	Caestre	19/02/1916	29/02/1916
Heading	113th. Brigade R.F.A. 25th. Divisional Artillery March 1916		
War Diary	Caestre	01/03/1916	09/03/1916
War Diary	Molinghem	10/03/1916	10/03/1916
War Diary	Heuchin	11/03/1916	17/03/1916
War Diary	Buneville	18/03/1916	31/03/1916
Heading	113th. Brigade R.F.A. 25th. Divisional Artillery April 1916		
War Diary	Buneville	03/04/1916	10/04/1916
War Diary	St. Michel	11/04/1916	24/04/1916
War Diary	Berthonval Farm	25/04/1916	30/04/1916
Heading	113th. Brigade R.F.A. 25th. Divisional Artillery May 1916		
War Diary	Berthonval Farm	01/05/1916	15/05/1916
War Diary	Capelle Fermont	23/05/1916	26/05/1916
War Diary	Berthonval Fm	27/05/1916	30/05/1916
War Diary	Capelle Fermont	31/05/1916	31/05/1916
Miscellaneous	Addenda		
Heading	113th. Brigade R.F.A. 25th. Divisional Artillery June 1916		
Miscellaneous	1/6 A.G's Office At the Base	06/07/1916	06/07/1916
War Diary	Capelle Fermont	01/06/1916	02/06/1916
War Diary	St. Michel	03/06/1916	15/06/1916
War Diary	Outrebois	16/05/1916	17/06/1916

War Diary	Villers Bocage	18/06/1916	19/06/1916
War Diary	Venette	20/06/1916	21/06/1916
War Diary	Plessis Brion	22/06/1916	24/06/1916
War Diary	St Leger	25/06/1916	30/06/1916
Miscellaneous	Nominal Roll Of Officers Of The 113th Brigade R.F.A.		
Heading	Headquarters, 113th Brigade, R.F.A. July 1916		
Miscellaneous	To Headquarters 25th Division A.	04/08/1916	04/08/1916
Miscellaneous	Staff Capt. M.G.C.	30/07/1916	30/07/1916
War Diary	St. Leger	01/07/1916	26/07/1916
Heading	113th. Brigade Royal Field Artillery August 1916		
War Diary	St Leger	01/08/1916	31/08/1916
Miscellaneous	Bois des Rigoles (ou Bois Carre)	14/04/1916	14/04/1916
Miscellaneous	Sur Le Bois Des Rigoles.		
Heading	113th. Brigade R.F.A. 25th. Divisional Artillery September 1916		
Miscellaneous	Staff Capt 25 D.A.	06/10/1916	06/10/1916
War Diary	St. Leger	01/09/1916	30/09/1916
Miscellaneous	Artillerie 53e Regiment	03/09/1916	03/09/1916
Miscellaneous	Programme des Tirs Pour la journee du 5 September	04/09/1916	04/09/1916
Miscellaneous	Le General Felineau Commandant La 162 Brigade Territoriale	05/09/1916	05/09/1916
Miscellaneous	Programme des tirs systematiques a executer les	05/09/1916	05/09/1916
Miscellaneous	Programme des tirs pour le 8 September.	06/09/1916	06/09/1916
Miscellaneous	Programme des Tirs pour le Neuf September	07/09/1916	07/09/1916
Miscellaneous	Note de Service	07/09/1916	07/09/1916
Miscellaneous	Programme Des Tirs pour la journee du 10 Septembre.	08/09/1916	08/09/1916
Miscellaneous	Programme Des Tirs pour le II Septembre	09/09/1916	09/09/1916
Miscellaneous	Programme Des Tirs pour la journee du 12 September	10/09/1916	10/09/1916
Miscellaneous	Additif au programme des Tirs pour la journee du 12 September 1916	11/09/1916	11/09/1916
Miscellaneous	Programme des Tirs pour la journee du 13 September	11/09/1916	11/09/1916
Miscellaneous	Artillerie 53e Regiment	12/09/1916	12/09/1916
Miscellaneous	Programme Des Tirs Pour La Journee Du 14 September.	12/09/1916	12/09/1916
Miscellaneous	Programme Des Tirs Pour La Journee Du 15 September.	13/09/1916	13/09/1916
Miscellaneous	Programme Des Tirs Pour La Journee Du 16 September.	14/09/1916	14/09/1916
Miscellaneous	Programme Des Tirs Pour La Journee Du 17 September	15/09/1916	15/09/1916
Miscellaneous	Programme Des Tirs Pour La Journee Du 18 September	16/09/1916	16/09/1916
Miscellaneous	Programme Des Tirs Pour La Journee Du 19 September	16/09/1916	16/09/1916
Miscellaneous	Programme Des Tirs Pour La Journee Du 20 September	16/09/1916	16/09/1916
Miscellaneous	Programme Des Tirs Pour La Journee Du 21 September		
Miscellaneous	Programme Des Tirs Pour La Journee Du 22 September	20/09/1916	20/09/1916
Miscellaneous	Programme Des Tirs Pour La Journee Du 23 September	21/09/1916	21/09/1916
Miscellaneous	Programme Des Tirs Pour La Journee Du 24 September	22/09/1916	22/09/1916
Miscellaneous	Programme Des Tirs Pour La Journee Du 25 September	21/09/1916	21/09/1916
Miscellaneous	Programme Des Tirs Pour La Journee Du 25 September	24/09/1916	24/09/1916
Miscellaneous	Order General No. 257	26/09/1916	26/09/1916
Heading	113th. Brigade R.F.A. 25th. Divisional Artillery October 1916		
War Diary	St. Leger Aux Bois Near Compiegne	02/10/1916	31/10/1916
Miscellaneous	IIIrd Armee Bde Corps d' Armies Artillery No. 6373	09/10/1916	09/10/1916
Miscellaneous	Adieux Du Colonel d'Alaqer De Costemok		
Miscellaneous	Order General No. 132	09/10/1916	09/10/1916
Operation(al) Order(s)	25th Divisional Artillery Operation Order No. 72	17/10/1916	17/10/1916

Miscellaneous	O.C. 110th Brigade R.F.A.	21/10/1916	21/10/1916
Miscellaneous	25th Divisional Artillery Operation Order No. 72		
Miscellaneous	25th Divisional Artillery Operation Order No. 72 Time Table For 18 Pdr Guns		
Miscellaneous	25th Divisional Artillery Operation Order No. 72		
Miscellaneous	Addendum No. 1 to 25th Divisional Arty Operation Order No. 72	18/10/1916	18/10/1916
Miscellaneous	Addendum No. 2 to 25th Div Arty O.O. 72	18/10/1916	18/10/1916
Miscellaneous	Addendum No. 3 to 25th Div Arty Operation Order No. 72	19/10/1916	19/10/1916
Heading	113th. Brigade R.F.A. 25th. Divisional Artillery November 1916		
War Diary	Mouquet Farm	01/11/1916	21/11/1916
War Diary	Usna Hill	22/11/1916	25/11/1916
War Diary	Monchy	26/11/1916	26/11/1916
War Diary	Cayeux	27/11/1916	30/11/1916
Heading	113th. Brigade R.F.A. 25th. Divisional Artillery December 1916		
War Diary	Romarin	01/12/1916	31/12/1916
Operation(al) Order(s)	25th Div. Artillery Order No. 86	30/11/1916	30/11/1916
Operation(al) Order(s)	36th Divisional Artillery Order No. 34	03/12/1916	03/12/1916
Operation(al) Order(s)	25th Divisional Artillery Order No. 87	04/12/1916	04/12/1916
Miscellaneous			
Operation(al) Order(s)	36th Divisional Artillery Order No. 57.	12/12/1916	12/12/1916
Miscellaneous	Bombardment Table.		
Operation(al) Order(s)	36th Divisional Artillery Order No. 38.	15/12/1916	15/12/1916
Operation(al) Order(s)	36th Divisional Artillery Order No. 90.	22/12/1916	22/12/1916
Heading	War Diary of 113th A.F.A Bde. for February 1917		
War Diary	B. 12 Central	01/01/1917	22/02/1917
War Diary	Neuve Eglise	22/02/1917	28/02/1917

WO/95/2234

1/2 113 Brigade Royal Field Artillery

25TH DIVISION
DIVL ARTILLERY

113TH BRIGADE R.F.A.
SEP 1915 - FEB 1917

(Became A Fld Art Bde to 2 Army)

WO/7594

25th Div^n

113th Bde: R.F.A.
Vol I

Sept. & Oct. 15

113th Brigade R.F.A.

Army Form C. 2118

WAR DIARY
or
INTELLIGENCE SUMMARY.
(Erase heading not required.)

Place	Date	Hour	Summary of Events and Information	Remarks and references to Appendices
Aldershot	25/9/15	7am	The Brigade entrained at Gort, riding Aldershot for Southampton	App I
Southampton	25 "	5pm	Embarked at Southampton strength 24 Officers 691 other ranks 630 horses 60 mules 16 4.5" Hows 48 4.5" Wagons. Nominal Roll of Officers App I	I Nominal roll of officers
Havre	26 "	1am	The Brigade arrived at Havre about 1am and disembarked at 7am and proceeded to rest camp where it remained the night	App II
Hingue Caestre	27 "	4am	The Brigade marched to the Railway Station and entrained at 7am	App III
	28 "	7pm	Detrained at CAESTRE and proceeded by march route to VIEUX BERQUIN and occupied billets in farms in the district	App IV
Caestre	29 "	10am	Proceed by march route to NIEPPE, the concentration area of 25th Divn, and relieved 65 Bde R.F.A. in position N of ARMENTIÈRES in the PLOEGSTEERT district. Brigade Headquarters was established at OOSTHOVE CORNER 1400 yards N.E. of NIEPPE	App V
Oosthove Corner	30/9/15 to 12/10/15		Occupied in improving position and telephone communication, and verifying registration taken over from 65 Brigade R.F.A.	App VI

Army Form C. 2118.

WAR DIARY
~~INTELLIGENCE SUMMARY.~~
(Erase heading not required.)

Place	Date	Hour	Summary of Events and Information	Remarks and references to Appendices
Oothove Corner	13/10/15		The 25" Divisional Artillery made a wrecking demolition on this date. The 113 Brigade was told in readiness to assist in case of retaliation. "D" Battery fired 20 rounds of Lyddite at enemy troops moving on the MESSINES-WARNETON road at a range of 6,600 yards with satisfactory results. The enemy did not retaliate to any extent except that from 3 to 3-30 p.m. a few rounds of H.E. fell near the position occupied by "A" Battery. No damage was done.	101
OOSTHOVE FM	14/10/15	10 am	6 Shell were fired in the direction of C/113 but no damage was done.	
	19.10.15		Lieut S.C. Shad took over the command of the Brigade Ammunition Column in place of Capt. C. Wilson posted to Divisional Ammunition Column.	
	20.10.15		Capt. McDonald A.D. went to Div. Art. Headquarters. Capt. L.N. Elliott took command of B Battery.	
	21.10.15		Lieut C.R.M. Hutchison transferred from the 1st Canadian Division, joined as Adjutant.	
	22.10.15		Emplacements were commenced in proximity to the front line trenches by	

A/Battery, for two more Howitzers at ST YVES. Also positions for two more Howitzers in the front line were selected, under divisional orders at LE GHEER, and work commenced of necessity temporarily, since if all firing, as throwing up of construction, had to be carried on at night, & all available men required.

Orders were also received on this day to select 2 more positions for Howitzers in the trenches behind lines ch. 102. These positions were selected, & B/Battery instructed to proceed with their construction. B battery was also of necessity relieved from Forward Observation duty.

Detailed descriptions of these emplacements will be given later. The following extract from Div. Art. Orders are given in explanation of sites selected by divisional artillery. "Guns thus sited are used:1. to breach the enemy's front parapet: thus blocking his front line trench on the flank of an attack 2. To cut wire immediately before the assault; 3. To engage machine guns that may be disclosed at the last moment, and 4. To follow the infantry to the enemy's front line trench as soon as this is captured."

25th Bat Mt. 22.10.15

It was also stated that if sufficient emplacements of an enemy attack eventual

WAR DIARY
or
INTELLIGENCE SUMMARY.
(Erase heading not required.)

Army Form C. 2118

Place	Date	Hour	Summary of Events and Information	Remarks and references to Appendices
	Oct		These forward emplacements would be occupied for defensive purposes. To facilitate the carrying out of above instructions sites for guns were selected as near as possible to roads which could be used in an advance, & it is not proposed to add the finishing touches until after these are allotted.	
	22 to 29		Batteries engaged in registering from an emergency position. This was very much hindered by misty weather.	O.A.
	29		The batteries of the brigade are in action to the West of the La Hutte — PLOEGSTEERT ARMENTIÈRES road, 3 miles North of Armentières.	

25th Hussars

113th Bde: R.F.A.
Vol 2

12/
7761

Nov. 15

Army Form C. 2118

WAR DIARY
or
INTELLIGENCE SUMMARY.

(Erase heading not required.)

Instructions regarding War Diaries and Intelligence Summaries are contained in F. S. Regs. Part II. and the Staff Manual respectively. Title pages will be prepared in manuscript.

113 Brigade RFA
25th Division
FROM 1.11.15 — 29.11.15

Place	Date	Hour	Summary of Events and Information	Remarks and references to Appendices
OOSTHOVE	NOV. 1-9		Very little artillery activity, mists and rain prevented any good observation. During the last nine days the country has assumed its usual condition of mud, and a good deal of work has to be done on rebuilding dug outs etc.	
	11		2Lt. W. E. Emerson joined the brigade from the Divisional Ammunition Column. He was attached to the Lt. Lymon Ct. for a day and was then sent to "C" Battery. Lieut H. J. Jackson joined as BAC in his place.	
	17		A divisional "Battle Practice" was held today. This consisted in H.Q. Div A.G. sending orders for an imaginary attack, and allotting different targets to the several brigades. 1 round only being fired at each target. The times between when orders were issued by Division + round fired were taken. This was 9½ minutes for the 113th Bde. (average).	
	23		Weather has been very misty and there has been little artillery action of any note. Lieuts. J. d'O. Murray + P.O.L. Williams joined Complet. They	

Army Form C. 2118

WAR DIARY
or
INTELLIGENCE SUMMARY.
(Erase heading not required.)

Place	Date	Hour	Summary of Events and Information	Remarks and references to Appendices
	24th	1.30 PM	They were accomodated for the night at Bn. Headquarters and attached to "C" Battery and "A" Battery respectively. Germans opened a retaliation of sorts on our front line trenches at ST YVES & LE GHEER, also on Hill 63 (Canadian Division area) at 1.45 our wireless station received a B.Q. call "German batteries active at O.34 a 7.6. O.33 & 3.8. Ordon O.27 a 4.7." "A" & "D" battery were ordered to fire 16 rds apiece or two of these which were within our range. Fire was opened within 4 minutes of the receipt of the aeroplane message. Naturally no direct observation was possible but on our target the aeroplane reported our shells were falling within the Z (25yds) circle. Two other batteries were also reported and dealt with. An extra allowance of 60 rds was allowed us from Div Arty. This German retaliation was probably due to the activity of the Canadians on our left, who, making too much facility of observation and concealment given to them by Hill 63 have been particularly agressive. Today was the first clear day we have had for some time.	✻ Sheet 28.S.W. 1/20,000
	25th	10AM	Another Divl Arty Battle practice was held today commencing at 10.A.M. etc	

Army Form C. 2118

WAR DIARY
or
INTELLIGENCE SUMMARY.
(Erase heading not required.)

Instructions regarding War Diaries and Intelligence Summaries are contained in F.S. Regs., Part II and the Staff Manual respectively. Title pages will be prepared in manuscript.

Place	Date	Hour	Summary of Events and Information	Remarks and references to Appendices
	23rd	6.0PM	lasted till 12.20. 19 Rds were expended. Time taken from receipt of Div: order to Battery opening fire 4.36 minutes (average). Four rounds fired with C.S.P. cartridges at DEULEMONT. (Report forwarded) (It is considered that the flash is invisible provided 6 feet of cover above the muzzle is improvised. The danger of missing C.S.P. cartridges with the ordinary cartridges was noted as a great quantity of very visible smoke is emitted.)	J: J:
	27th		Unusual activity of German aircraft.	
	28th		Again German aircraft unusually active. They passed repeatedly over our lines, eventually driven away by our own aeroplanes.	J:
	29th		Weather changed, frost broken, rain. C. & D batteries carried out registrations on German front line trench in vicinity of FACTORY FARM. U15d.10.3.	Sheet 28.S.W. J:

113th Bde. RFA.
Vol 3

D/7936

25th RFA

Army Form C. 2118

A Bos 113th Bde. R.F.A.
25th Div'n

WAR DIARY
or
INTELLIGENCE/SUMMARY.

(Erase heading not required.)

Instructions regarding War Diaries and Intelligence Summaries are contained in F. S. Regs., Part II. and the Staff Manual respectively. Title pages will be prepared in manuscript.

Place	Date	Hour	Summary of Events and Information	Remarks and references to Appendices
OOSTHOVE NIEPPE X	Dec 1/5		There has been nothing unusual to report, the Germans have been very quiet these last few days	#/20,000 Sheet 36 N.W.
Ma. B11c 10.n.	6th	4.	A German heavy gun about 15 cm. shelled the road about of NIEPPE at 8.30 p.m today. The shells first two or three shells fell harmlessly about 400-500 yds from C Battery's wagon line. The Germans suddenly dropped three shells and one put the first of four shells into one of the huts where the drivers of C Battery were having their tea. The shell upset the brazier & set the hut on fire, killing 2 men outright, 18 others were evacuated, but they were all removed from the burning hut in time. 3 of these 18 died in hospital, 9 were only slightly wounded and remained with the battery. C.By. removed its other wagon line as it was thought to be a fairly accidental one, but as the Germans continued to fire shells for several hours C Battery were moved to B Battery's wagon line where this was vacated. O.A.	
	7th		The G.O.C 2nd Army and staff visited B Battery's wagon line at 3.30. They were to have inspected the B.A.C. as well but appeared to have no efficient mind for to get round. The wagon line at all without molestation through most 12 inches deep in spots of late having been swept for three days	

2353 W. W2544/1454 700,000 5/15 D.D.&L. A.D.S.S./Forms/C. 2118.

WAR DIARY
or
INTELLIGENCE SUMMARY.

(Erase heading not required.)

Army Form C. 211

Place	Date	Hour	Summary of Events and Information	Remarks and references to Appendices
	Dec 7th		previously.	
	8th		The O.C. Lands. Fusiliers organised preparations for an attack at night on a portion of the German trenches N. of FRELINGHIEN. The 113th Bde. were to cooperate & fire in all 370 rounds of lyddite at night. The operation was 1½ hour later placed on the night of the 8th-9th. But the O.C. operations considered it too late for the purpose & the attack was postponed until the following night.	Reference Map ½ 1/20,000 Sheet 36 N.W. CA
	9-10th	11.30 PM 2.30 AM	Batteries were ordered to stand to for above operation at 11:30 PM. The night was boisterous, with rain & clear intervals. At 2.30 A.M. 10th, orders were received that operation were abandoned. Lient Lamb was posted to B. Bty & Lient Somerville Smith posts to G. Bty from B Bty.	
	11th		A machine gun emplacement reported by the infantry was successfully dealt with by C Battery. 8/113 was withdrawn out of action to billets near STEENWERCK preparatory to their transfer. Capt Elliot R.F.A, who had been in command of 8/113 since Capt MacLeod (?) left for a instruction for Bde Maj. at H.Q.R.A 25th Div, was transferred to No.3 Section C.A.C. The command of 8/113	
	12th		was temporarily handed over to Lieut Dobell. at LE TOUQUET C.10 B.	CA 1/20,000 Sheet 36 N.W.
	13th		The German salient being almost enfilade cut effectively out effectively today by the divisional artillery and the 9.2" Howitzers. The Germans it was understood used the houses in this salient as their bomb-proof shelters. A.C & D batteries 113/Bde Fire bombarded the front line trenches. Several Germans were seen to leave their front trenches & make for the houses in LE TOUQUET. They were followed and for ¾ of an hour from 11.15 - 12 Noon the houses were bombarded. Considerable material damage being caused. The houses however	

WAR DIARY or INTELLIGENCE SUMMARY

Army Form C. 2118

Place	Date	Hour	Summary of Events and Information	Remarks and references to Appendices
	Dec			
	15th		Air probably provided with bombing of billets, was a by Lt. H.Q. HQrs. will have been sent.	
	16th		Warning received from Corps of probability of Ger attack. Reinforced later.	
			Heavy fire by division on our night during night. German retaliate about 2.30 A.M. Our division opened to their had a suppressed delivery artillery several positions.	
	17th	8.30 A.M.	"B" Battery left for us to be a sent to the Lahore Divisional Battery, at present supporting the 2nd Canadian Division on our right. The following officers left with the Battery. Lieut L Dobell, Lieut G H Lambe, Lieut L S Johnson. A section was also sent from our Bde Ammn Col consisting of 1 NCO and together with its officer who left us was Lieut W J Jackson, 4 wagons, 12 draught horses & 11 mules & 3 riders were sent with this section. draught mules & 3 riders were sent with this section. Battle practice was held between 9.30 A.M. & 12 Noon.	
	20th	2 P.M.	Trench mortar batteries etc fired about 200 rounds into a German work constructed recently at the end of a sap at U.99.a.4.6 "D" Battery (1 section) was ordered 25 rds to co-operate with above firings. Bombardment lasted 1 hour. Considerable damage was done to the German work by the Trench mortars, which compared with no relation in asperity to the Germans. I think them comparatively due to it being a regimental day. on the 2nd of the Germans artillery observed in their own front trenches. B.G.C.R.A. took advantage of this operations to put on 18 pr. Gun about 300 yds behind our own Trenches to fire	1/25000 Sheet 28SW

WAR DIARY
or
INTELLIGENCE SUMMARY.
(Erase heading not required.)

Army Form C. 2118

Place	Date	Hour	Summary of Events and Information	Remarks and references to Appendices
			about 30 yds with the sights set for close range. Four guns etc. in order to test the accuracy of figures used at short range. One artillery officer adviser was prepared at LE GHEER + an officer in an O.P. about 600 yds to the right of Touquet, the sights being fixed even if own bearing could be taken to the muzzle of the shot. Our infantry were even if our aplan in safest places. It is considered that no figure will miss long accurate at short range. C.A.	
	21st	9.30 P.M	At D Battery Gun position the sentry noticed a man poking about in party No 76m platform. This man was challenged. He answered something unintelligibly when the sentry advanced to investigate he turned and fled again the road towards PLOEGSTEERT, Deepcut + fired as before through gaps which apparently were very well. The sentry followed him but found the 3/4 stand of a hound wire fence which the man had cleared quickly but lost him. This man's face was not seen. Particulars as to height abouts are reported to A.P.M. C.A.	
	22nd	10 PM	Another man probably the same as above was seen at the end of 6 fields the firing was turned out and he was stalked, one sentry got within rifled of him when he was challenged. Ordered by H.Q. to put 200 rounds daily into Burlegs H.q which is to say just after dark. All three batteries to take part. C.S.P. ammunition is being sent along as it is available. C.A.	

2353 Wt. W2344/1454 700,000 5/15 D. D. & L. A.D.S.S./Forms/C. 2118.

WAR DIARY or INTELLIGENCE SUMMARY.

(Erase heading not required.)

Army Form C. 2118.

Instructions regarding War Diaries and Intelligence Summaries are contained in F. S. Regs., Part II. and the Staff Manual respectively. Title pages will be prepared in manuscript.

Place	Date	Hour	Summary of Events and Information	Remarks and references to Appendices
	23		The division were to have been out 8 months, have now Mobilised for 8 days leave. 5 at a.m. this morning	
	24		Battle Practice 9.30 A.M. to 12.30 P.M. Shelled Thick Path Practice ordered for every one for the purpose of testing ammunition.	
	25		Xmas day. No activity on our front at all.	
	26		Obtained sanction from division authority for the replenishment of Shrapnel. This had previously been refused for, with what some call very nearly reason - down. Lyddite 450 per gun Shrapnel	
	27		Trench Mortars ordered to bombard Railway Junction. Junction timed for 2.30 P.M. & Trench Mortar "A" Battery cooperated & fired 40 r.p. Guns were very slow, 30 rounds only was ordered. The day was very clear, so ought what an observer was carried out as ordered...	

Place	Date	Hour	Summary of Events and Information	Remarks and references to Appendices
	29th		time to prepare the necessary platforms for their guns. Aeroplane shoot on German Battery failed to come off owing to confusion in registration, one 18 pr. Battery also shot on the target which Canadian Heavy Battery was attempting to register. Wireless stations in Division area both have the same call.	
	30th		Mud in A Battery's wagon line 24" deep, new field found for parking Amm. wagons as it is impossible to get wagons out in a hurry, without danger of suffocation to an any horse which came down.	

J. Anderson
Col. R.F.A.
Comd'g 113th Brigade R.F.A.

113th. BRIGADE R. F. A.

25th. DIVISIONAL ARTILLERY

J A N U A R Y   1 9 1 6.

Army Form C. 2118.

WAR DIARY
or
INTELLIGENCE SUMMARY.
(Erase heading not required.)

H.Qrs 113th Bde. R.F.A
25th Division

Place	Date 1916	Hour	Summary of Events and Information	Remarks and references to Appendices
DOSTHOVE NIEPPE. B 11 C 10.4	Jan 1-5		Nothing important to report. Weather keeping a little finer and mud consequently drying up a little. Reports of gas on German front, but Westerly winds constant. JA	#1/20000 Sheet 36 N.W.
	6th		Battle practice. O.C. 113rd Bde. had to conduct battle practice. Decided to rebuild observation station at LE GHEER Estaminet, owing to scheme again being brought forward to bombard and take "BIRDCAGE". Observation stations in St YVES and at LE GHEER feverishly reconstructed & strengthened in consequence. A slit for observation purposes was constructed out of 4 loophole plates made in pairs set at an angle of 85 degrees 85° + a gap of 1¾ inches for observation purposes. This slit was very easy to lift conceal with some dirty straw lying on the rafters, + affords an excellent view + protection. LE GHEER ESTAMINET is some 250 yds from German trenches. JA	
	10th		Watering of horses commenced today. "D" Battery were all mollumia, the B.A.C. supplying them with any necessary teams for fatigues. Inoculation done with very much reduced dose on horses eyelid. Effects said to be all over in 48 hours. Precautions against gas attacks very strictly enforced, possible gas attack if wind changes, expected. JA	
	11th		All vehicles now marked with Division sign. Very little activity on both sides, but Germans a little jumpy at night. JA	

Army Form C. 2118.

WAR DIARY
or
INTELLIGENCE SUMMARY.
(Erase heading not required.)

Place	Date	Hour	Summary of Events and Information	Remarks and references to Appendices
	JAN 13th		Secret instruction received about scheme for occupying the LE TOUQUET Salient for a short period by the infantry. Preliminary orders received. Generally — 1. Task of 118th Bde is to Breach parapet where infantry want to enter German trenches. 2. Bombard Support trenches during general bombardment. 3. Bombard flanks of locality to be entered by infantry. It is proposed to use gas on left of operations, & smoke to cover infantry advance. Scheme includes cooperation of 9.2" & 12" Howitzers, one detail seems to have been omitted as yet, namely no provision seems to have been made for dealing with hostile observing stations. There are better ones for this locality, & several known situated 1000 - 1550 yds behind LE TOUQUET an known obs. stas. & a very accurate retaliatory fire could be directed from these on our position.	C.A.
	14th to 16th		Very busy ensuring communications & observing sta. for above Scheme. (Several decisions seem to have attached 1 Hour. batty to each 18 pr. Bde. using a group system. If this had been in force with 25th Div. The task of obtaining efficient communication for Howitzer batteries would have been very difficult. Also, emplacements under separate Bde. system are of course constructed to cover whole division front. There we were able to concentrate fire on LE TOUQUET which is situated on extreme left of 25th Div. line without any difficulty whatsoever.) Communications for "A" & "D" batteries are very long, & the disadvantage of having batteries so far apart was noted. It is considered, as 4.5 Howitzers are so scarce that an effort will be made to concentrate howitzers in future, & they are invariably all required for close "shooting for every scheme.	

WAR DIARY
or
INTELLIGENCE SUMMARY.

(Erase heading not required.)

Army Form C. 2118.

Place	Date	Hour	Summary of Events and Information	Remarks and references to Appendices
	17th		Sufficient telephone wire for the necessary alternative circuits is never obtainable, whereas if batteries were concentrated this would be feasible. C.S.	
			Detailed instructions have been received, it is impossible to enumerate scheme, 17 sheets of foolscap have been received. Briefly scheme is as follows:-	
			(a) 1.30 - 3.0 P.M. Parapet to be tackled by howitzers, wire to be cut by 18 prs.	
			(b) 3.0 P.M. Heavy Artillery commence registering + bombardment.	
			(c) 3.30 - 4.40 P.M. General bombardment.	
			(d) 4.30 P.M. Gas to be let loose from trenches 97-101.	
			(e) 5.37 P.M. Smoke to be let loose from BARKENHAM FARM. (C10 b 4.2.)* South wards + from Railway crossing leading C11 s 7. Attack by infantry (7th Batt) to take place under cover of this. Royal Irish Rifles lately come from 3rd Div. were detailed for this.	*½ cross B. Sheet 36 N.W.
			(f) 4.40 P.M. Heavy Artillery + Trench Mortars to crossfire + smaller calibres to left of Salient.	
			(g) 4.45 P.M. Infantry assault.	
			(h) 5.15 P.M. Infantry to return to our own trenches. Barrages to be maintained.	
			113 Bde. R.F.A. 1.30 P.M. onwards. "C" Batty to reach parapet at C10 b 4½. 5½. + C10 b 3½. 2½. 50 Rds. H.E. each	(Sg. by.)
			2.0 - 2.30 P.M. A + D may register of necessary on C10 b 6a - C10 b 8½ 9½ + C10 b 5 6 - C10 b 6.3.	
			2.30 - 3.0 P.M. D may register of necessary on C10 b 6.7½ - C10 b 10.5 + C10 b 5½ 8½ - C10 b 8½.4.	
			3.30 - 4.40 P.M. "C" Bty to bombard with one section C10 b 6.7½ - C10 b 10.5 errat Amm. allotted 50 H.E.	
			3.50 - 4.40 P.M. D "Bty to bombard 1 Gun C10 b 6.7½ - C10 b 10.5 50 Rds. H.E. 1 Gun C10 b 5½ 8½ to C10 b 8½.4 50 Rds. H.E. 2 Guns C10 b 5.6 to C10 b 6.3. 75 Shrapnel.	
			C10 b 6.7½ - C10 b 10.5 A.D.S.S./Forms/C. 2118.	

WAR DIARY or INTELLIGENCE SUMMARY

Army Form C. 2118.

Place	Date	Hour	Summary of Events and Information	Remarks and references to Appendices
	18th		3.50 – 4.40 P.M. "A" Bty to bombard C10 b 6.2 to C10 d 8.4, 9.2. Amm. 100 rds. H.E.	
			At 4.40 P.M. to 4.50 P.M. + again at 5.0 P.M. to 5.20 P.M.	
			"A" Bty to bombard C11 c 5.6 50 rds. H.E.	
			"D" Bty to bombard C4 d 2½. 3½ 30 rds H.E.	
			Each battery to have 100 rds H.E. ammn and about, available for counter battery work.	
	19th	1.30 A.M.	Orders received operation to be carried out on 19th if not orders to contrary were received from Div H.Qrs. by At.	
		10 A.M.	Communications all tested by 9 A.M. registrations had all been completed by Noon 18th inst. Div. Order. Operations were to be carried out without smoke or gas if wind changed. At 10.0 A.M. wind light + shifting – find night for us.	
		(9 P.M.)	Wirecutting commenced at 12 Noon, + soon afterwards German retaliation began to seriously interfere with all communications. "A" + "C" Battery commanding decided 12.30 P.M. to verify their registrations before all communications gave out. A wire tried 3 ft dump from Le Touquet Station to front line was one of the first to be cut. Registrations were verified + found accurate. German retaliation became so heavy soon after the trench mortars opened fire that it was soon seen that communication with front line observing stations had not much chance of surviving. 18 prs battery were opposite C10 b 3½. 3½. soon lost communication. German wire was cut almost entirely by Trench Mortar Batteries firing from front line trenches. Four hours collapsed onto communication trench between LE TOUQUET and BARKENHAM FARM. The breaching operations carried out by C Battery were very successful, the parapet was breached, + also considerable damage was also reported done to wire mentioned above. On the S. side of the salient the wire was successfully cut by 112th Bde. R.F.A. 18 prs.	

Army Form C. 2118.

WAR DIARY
or
INTELLIGENCE SUMMARY.
(Erase heading not required.)

Place	Date	Hour	Summary of Events and Information	Remarks and references to Appendices
			whose permanent S.O.S. line was the only one which remained intact. The bombardments were carried out entirely from regulations & were reported accurate as far as could be seen through smoke etc. The guns were shooting very well off their previous registrations. Communication from LE TOUQUET Station Obs. Sta. was maintained but none of front trench lines survived. Messages had to be taken back by orderlies to "H" Station. Sct Programme was carried out exactly as ordered.	C.H.
		2.33 P.M.	Div. ordered fire on some guns reported to be just S. of bridge at FRELINGHIEN C11 c. 3.8. "A" Bty fired 25 rds H.E. at this target. General effect was observed & reported satisfactory but messages could not be got back to Battery in time to give corrections.	
		3.28 P.M.	Buildings at C11 c. 7½ and C11 c. 7½.1 reported through Div. Arty to be observing stations engaged by "A" Bty 40 rounds A.E. (unobserved)	
		3.55 P.M.	"C" Battery fired 25 rds H.E. at a battery reported by D.H.Q. at U28 d 6.9. between two buildings	
		4.35 P.M.	From 4.35 P.M. – 4.50 P.M. instructions from C.R.A.	
			C. 6. c. 2. 3.	
		5.39	"D" Battery fired 25 rds. H.E. at battery reported at U29 a 6.8. incl. C.P.A. 5.16 P.M. – 5.20 P.M. "D" Battery fired 40 rds H.E. at battery at	
		6.45.	"A" Battery fired 30 rds. at guns at FRELINGHIEN BRIDGE. C11 c. 5.8.	
			Total ammunition expended 656 B.X and 75 B.	C.H.

Army Form C. 2118.

WAR DIARY
or
INTELLIGENCE SUMMARY.
(Erase heading not required.)

Instructions regarding War Diaries and Intelligence Summaries are contained in F.S. Regs., Part II. and the Staff Manual respectively. Title pages will be prepared in manuscript.

Place	Date	Hour	Summary of Events and Information	Remarks and references to Appendices
	Jan. 19th to 25th		The Germans attempted very little retaliation for operations of 18th and there was very little artillery activity between dates mentioned in margin. NIEPPE was occasionally shelled by the same guns as casualties in "C" Battery, major hours.	C.F.
	25th		MOVE TO REST AREA. When orders for the move were received it was found that owing to the 9th Div. having the Howitzers attached to each 18 pr. Bde. according to the group system (happily not favoured by 25th Div.), that half a battery or Bde A mm Col. moved every try of the 6 days taken for the move. Half of the 18 pr. Bde. concerned of course moved on the same day. An interval of an hour was allowed between the times allotted for each half unit to march. See extracts from marching orders attd (appendix I.) 113th Bde half unit was allotted the last time in each case which meant every as of our units almost after dark. This appeared unnecessary & meant discomfort.	C.F.
EECKE.	31st		Move carried out without difficulty or trouble, units managed to get to billets before dark. Bde. H.Qrs. came here today.	C.F.

Lawrance
Col. R.F.A.
Com'd'g 113th Brigade R.F.A.

APPENDIX I

From O.C. 113 Bde. R.F.A
To O.C. B.A.C./113.
    A. C. & D. Btys.

The following extracts from marching orders are given for information:—

Jan 26th

V. { ½ of B.A.C. "A" "B" "C" "D" 112 Bde head of columns to reach PONT d'ACHELLES at 9.0, 9.30, 10.30, 11.30 A.M. & 12.30 P.M. respectively.

then:—

½ C/113 Head of column to pass PONT d'ACHELLES (B8a.6.6.) at 1.30 P.M.

Jan 27th Same as above

Jan 28th V { .... Same as Jan 26th for 111th Bde.

then:—

½ B.A.C. 113 Head of column to pass PONT d'ACHELLES (B8a.6.6.) at 1.30 P.M.

½ D/113 Head of column to pass PONT d'ACHELLES (B8a.6.6.) at 2.30 P.M.

Jan 29th Same as for Jan 29th

Jan 30th V{ ... Same as Jan 26th for
110th Bde. But all units start
1 hour earlier.
then :-
½ A/113 Head of column to pass
PONT d'ACHELLES (B 8 a 6.6.) at 12.30 P.M.

Jan 31st Same as for Jan 30th

A party of one officer and four NCO's or
men will be left behind to do any
clearing up necessary and also to go
through all lines after units have left to
ensure that positions have been left clean.
This party will follow after unit as soon
as task is finished.

A tracing of a 1/20,000 map is attached
the area can be located from 1/100000 HAZEBROUCK
Sheet 5A. Tracing shows positions of
billets. These are correct. They differ in
one or two cases from Map references of billets
supplied by R.A. HQrs.

C. R. M. Hutchison
Lieut
RE

24.1.16.

113th. BRIGADE R. F. A.

25th. DIVISIONAL ARTILLERY

F E B R U A R Y 1 9 1 6.

Army Form C. 2118.

WAR DIARY
or
INTELLIGENCE SUMMARY.

(Erase heading not required.)

HQrs. 113th Bde. R.F.A.
25th DIVISION

Place	Date 1916 FEB.	Hour	Summary of Events and Information	Remarks and references to Appendices
EECKE	1st to 3rd		During this period units were left to slaughter stores etc. and as far as possible afternoons were kept absolutely free for recreation. Subsection football matches were arranged to carry on every afternoon. Subsection marches within units were very keenly contested, & they were the great advantage of giving the maximum No. of men of a unit a game. Battery matches were also arranged for, but unfortunately weather	J.A.
	3rd		move to WATTEN training area cut these out. 2 Lieut F.M. Walsh joined the Bde. & was posted to C Battery.	J.A.
VOLKERINCKHOVE	4th		The Bde. marched as a Bde. to VOLKERINCKHOVE in WATTEN training area.	J.A.
	10th		2 Lt. L. Wise R.F.A. (T.) was posted to the 113th Bde. & was posted to C Battery. Other officers joined on the same date but were posted elsewhere in the 6th Div. Training was carried out according to programme attached (Appendix I.)	J.A.
	4-14			
	11th		D Battery was sent with 9 18/pr batteries to reinforce the line East of ARMENTIERES & was attached to 21st Divl Arty.	J.A.
	12th		The Army Commander inspected the Bde. and expressed himself as very pleased with all he saw.	W.T.
EECKE	14th		The Bde. returned to EECKE rest area.	e/c

Army Form C. 2118.

WAR DIARY
or
INTELLIGENCE SUMMARY.
(Erase heading not required.)

Instructions regarding War Diaries and Intelligence Summaries are contained in F.S. Regs., Part II. and the Staff Manual respectively. Title pages will be prepared in manuscript.

Place	Date	Hour	Summary of Events and Information	Remarks and references to Appendices
ECKE	Feb 18th		Received notification that we were out of 25th Div. area, & that we would have to move. This is annoying as previous to occupation of these billets the R.A.4 Gus had been asked if area was within our own, & had given a satisfactory answer. (This has been experienced before.)	
CAESTRE	19th		"A" & "C" Batteries on R.A.C. area billeted round FRAMECAES H.Qrs. in village of CAESTRE	
	19th to 29th		Two Bde. Adj. Tactical Schemes were carried out, but several orders to be ready to move at short notice were received. "D"	
	29th		"D" Battery ordered to return. Div. is under orders to move at 9 hours notice.	
			N.B. During this period all the guns except D. 1 of D Batteries & 1 of A Battery were taken down & overhauled by I.O.M. BAILLEUL & found by him to be in very good condition.	

J. Newton
....
Col. R.F.A.
Comd'g 110th Brigade R.F.A.

25th. DIVISIONAL ARTILLERY

113th. BRIGADE R. F. A.

25th. DIVISIONAL ARTILLERY

M A R C H   1 9 1 6.

WAR DIARY
or
INTELLIGENCE SUMMARY.
(Erase heading not required.)

Army Form C. 2118.

H. Ord. 113th Bde. R.F.A.

25th Dec.

Place	Date 1916 MARCH	Hour	Summary of Events and Information	Remarks and references to Appendices
CAESTRE	1st to 9th		Rumours give our destination as ARRAS but no official notification received. Ordered to move tomorrow early to clear HAZEBROUCK by 8.30 A.M. Commander in chief is to inspect us on our way through. 2Lt. J.G. Howell left to join Flying Corps.	C.A.
MOLINGHEM	10th		Started 6.15 a.m. this morning, snow + frequent. March very orderly and exiting satisfactory. One G.S wagon only, was stuck in ditch at very difficult place, but arrived here by 6 P.M. Billeting very easy + comfortable. Splendid by farms available. Commander in chief did not inspect us.	C.A.
HEUCHIN	11th		Left MOLINGHEM. 8.15 A.M. Cold, but fine. Billeting very difficult at HEUCHIN. Village previously rest billet of french troops. Barns very much broken down + very little decent accommodation for men + horses available. A Battery horses put in village square.	C.A.
	14th		2/Lts. P.K. Ironside, G.R.G. Alston, G.H. Fraser joined from D.A.C. 2Lieut L. McEwan reported evacuated to Base hospital. Lt. C.R.M. Hutchison, ordered to join 7th Division (act as Capt. pending promotion.) Lt. F.H.S. Pownall took over duties of adjutant.	C.A.

Army Form C. 2118.

WAR DIARY
or
INTELLIGENCE SUMMARY.
(Erase heading not required.)

Place	Date	Hour	Summary of Events and Information	Remarks and references to Appendices
	March			
HEUCHIN	16.	—	Received orders to move tomorrow morning at 9.15 A.M. Destination BUNEVILLE - which is about 5 miles S. of ST. POL, we shall be very sorry to leave Heuchin. MKP.	
	17.		Brigade marched out of HEUCHIN at 9.15 P.M. LT. HUTCHISON came with us as far as ANVIN, where he entrained for MERICOURT. During the march verbal messages received that one Battery must be prepared to move tonight - 'D' Battery detailed - Brigade arrived BUNEVILLE at 2.15 P.M. Quite a small village + very dirty and insanitary - Barns etc. have been badly knocked about by French troops - No British troops been here before - Billeting bad - Very little accommodation for men, no straw to be obtained locally - Horses - all outside in the fields - Watering - very bad - only one pool in the village + horses will hardly touch that. MKP.	
BUNEVILLE	18. to 25.		Spent most of our time cleaning up + endeavouring to make the place sanitary - Horses have to go to MAGINCOURT for water distance 3½ miles.	

WAR DIARY
or
INTELLIGENCE SUMMARY

Army Form C. 2118.

Place	Date	Hour	Summary of Events and Information	Remarks and references to Appendices
BUNEVILLE	March 18 to 25		Leave started again on the 19th. 'D' Battery left us on morning of the 20th destination SAVY. They went into billets & stayed there until they had completed the Bty. position and the Wagon lines. Although we were informed that billets had been arranged for them - when they arrived nothing was ready at all. On the 22nd 2 Lieut L. MacEwan rejoined the Brigade from Hospital. On the 21st Lieut J. Schooling joined the Bde. on posting from the 122nd Bde. R.F.A. On the 23rd he got orders to move to FLERS, about 5 miles W. of BUNEVILLE - went over here & fixed up billets etc. Move was cancelled at midnight 23rd-24th. On the 24th one section of the B.A.C. joined 'D' Battery. We are now in the XVII Corps - 3rd Army - 'D' Battery is attached to the 23rd Hy. Bde. R.G.A.	

WAR DIARY
or
INTELLIGENCE SUMMARY
(Erase heading not required.)

Place	Date	Hour	Summary of Events and Information	Remarks and references to Appendices
BUNEVILLE	March 26 to 31.		We are building 7158 turning an empty house into a Bathing Place for the Brigade. Close to the same house there is a well which supplies Brick good water. We have taken a 60 ft. water trough - which was in the middle of the village - down there & are filling it from the well - The well being very deep (120 ft. to level of the water) it is a very slow business. 2 Lieut Gibbon joined from the B.A.C. on the 30th posted to 'C' Batty. 2 Lieut. Jennings joined from B.A.C. on the 31st and is posted to Bde - H.Qrs - On the 31st the C. in C. inspected the troops of the 25th Division. The 113th Bde. R.F.A. considers that he, inspected the C. in C. around him he certainly looked at him much more than he looked at us -	7158

25th. DIVISIONAL ARTILLERY

113th. BRIGADE R. F. A.

25th. DIVISIONAL ARTILLERY

A P R I L   1 9 1 6.

113 Bn R ?
Vol 6

Army Form C. 2118.

WAR DIARY
~~INTELLIGENCE SUMMARY~~
(Erase heading not required.)

Instructions regarding War Diaries and Intelligence Summaries are contained in F.S. Regs, Part II. and the Staff Manual respectively. Title pages will be prepared in manuscript.

Place	Date	Hour	Summary of Events and Information	Remarks and references to Appendices
BUNEVILLE	APRIL 3rd		2 Lieut A.E. Gates joined the Brigade on posting from Ireland. He is posted to the Bde. Amm. Column.	
"	4th to 7th		Weather is beautiful. We are still engaged in cleaning up the village.	
"	8th		We were informed this morning by the CRA that the Brigade would move as early as possible to Grand Camp, St. Michel. This place is about 5 miles to the N. of Buneville. We shall go under canvas. Nothing ready at all at present.	
"	9th		Went over to inspect the site of our future camp - seems very nice, big field in the midst of the St. Michel woods - Promised the D.A.A. & QMG to move in on Tuesday he 11th - As nothing is ready, this does not leave us too much time.	
"	10th		Busy getting the camp fixed up. The R.E. are putting up 4 wooden huts for us. We have	

Army Form C. 2118.

WAR DIARY
or
INTELLIGENCE SUMMARY.
(Erase heading not required.)

Place	Date	Hour	Summary of Events and Information	Remarks and references to Appendices
BUNEVILLE	APRIL 10th		also been given 5 Bell Tents and 190 waterproof sheets (each sheet measuring 12' x 9') for bivouacs. That is all - 2 Lieut. L. MacEwan was evacuated to-day with jaundice -	
ST. MICHEL	11th		The Brigade (less 'D' Battery and 1 section of the B.A.C.) marched out of BUNEVILLE at 9 A.M. Of course it was raining; it always does rain when this Brigade moves anywhere. It has rained practically the whole day. It is bad luck, this being out first day in the new camp - If we could only have had the ground dry to pitch our bivouacs on! -	
"	14th		It has rained solidly since we arrived here. The mud is becoming rather appalling. Consider in everything the men are keeping very well. Horses look very wretched.	
"	15th		3 Officers and 70 men have gone up to work on the Corps Line - he have to prepare 2 4.5 How: Battery positions -	

Army Form C. 2118.

WAR DIARY
or
INTELLIGENCE SUMMARY.
(Erase heading not required.)

Instructions regarding War Diaries and Intelligence Summaries are contained in F. S. Regs., Part II. and the Staff Manual respectively. Title pages will be prepared in manuscript.

Place	Date	Hour	Summary of Events and Information	Remarks and references to Appendices
ST. MICHEL	APRIL 18	—	We are going to relieve the 46th Division (T) Relief orders were issued from this office to-day to all Batteries and the Bde. The relief of the Artillery extends over three nights, April 23/24, 24/25 and 25/26. As regards this Brigade we are effecting the reliefs on the nights of the 23/24 and 25/26. The Method of Relief is as follows:— One Section of each Battery will march on April 23. to their new wagon lines and they will relieve one section of the Battery of the 46 Divl. Arty. that same night, April 23/24. The remaining Section of each Battery will march on the 25. April to their wagon lines and relieve the remaining section of the Bty. of the 46 Divl. Arty. that same night. The R.O. and Brigade H.Q. march to their new billets on 25. April. We are taking over from the 4th N. Mid. Howitzer Bde. Battery Commanders and Six Telephonists are going to the attached to the Battery they are relieving	

Army Form C. 2118.

WAR DIARY
or
INTELLIGENCE SUMMARY
(Erase heading not required.)

Place	Date	Hour	Summary of Events and Information	Remarks and references to Appendices
ST. MICHEL	April 18/5		from the 21. April with a view to making themselves familiar with all communications etc. "D" Battery, who have been in action and attached to the 23rd Heavy Brigade R.G.A. for Counter Battery Work since March 20 - will of course rejoin us - They are moving into a new position on the nights of April 23/24 and 25/26 (just the same as the other two Batteries of the Brigade. Their new position is only about 300ˣ distant from the one they occupy at present - Batteries whom we are relieving — "R" Battery (A/113) 2nd Derby Battery (B/113) 1st Derby Battery (C/113)	
"	19/5		At BERTHONVAL FM., 5th future Brigade HQ., (here is a large Artillery Telephone Exchange (about 25 lines) 2 Lieut. Jennings, who has been appointed Brigade Signalling Officer, went up here today to take over the Exchange. He will stay here until we arrive.	

Army Form C. 2118.

WAR DIARY
or
INTELLIGENCE SUMMARY.
(Erase heading not required.)

Instructions regarding War Diaries and Intelligence Summaries are contained in F. S. Regs., Part II. and the Staff Manual respectively. Title pages will be prepared in manuscript.

Place	Date	Hour	Summary of Events and Information	Remarks and references to Appendices
ST. MICHEL	APRIL 22nd		2 Lieut. A. E. Gates has been attached to 'A' Battery –	
"	23rd		One section from 'A' and one from 'C' Battery marched out from here at 8.30 AM.	
"	24th		At about 8 PM this evening we were informed by the R.A. Office that it had been discovered that the villages in which the Rally; Wagon lines were situated were much too congested, and that this Brigade must move all its wagon lines to CAPELLE-FERMONT – The Colonel is going on to reconnoitre the place early to-morrow –	
BERTHONVAL FARM	25th		The remaining sections of 'A' and 'C' Batteries, the R.Q. and Brigade HQ marched out of ST. MICHEL at 8 AM this morning. CAPELLE-FERMONT moving all night, the R.Q. and Brigade HQ settled down here immediately. The Batteries will move their wagon lines here on the 27th.	

2353 Wt. W2514/1454 700,000 5/15 D.D.&L. A.D.S.S./Forms/C. 2118.

Army Form C. 2118.

WAR DIARY
or
INTELLIGENCE SUMMARY.
(Erase heading not required.)

Instructions regarding War Diaries and Intelligence Summaries are contained in F. S. Regs., Part II. and the Staff Manual respectively. Title pages will be prepared in manuscript.

Place	Date	Hour	Summary of Events and Information	Remarks and references to Appendices
BERTHONVAL FARM.	APRIL 25/4		The Relief of the 4th N.M. Howitzer Bde. was carried out successfully and was complete by 9 P.M. At midday to-day the enemy exploded a mine opposite the end of BOYAU CENTRALE.	
"	26/4		Early this morning, at about 3.30 AM, the enemy blew up two mines in front of trench Q.90. During the night of the 25/26 "A" Battery fired 290 rounds H.E. at the new craters at the end of BOYAU CENTRALE.	
"	27/4		Quiet during the day.	
"	28/4		The enemy blew up a mine just to the north of the crater opposite the end of BOYAU CENTRALE at 7.30 PM to-day. A hostile Battery was located the other day, this morning at 11.30½ AM, all the Batteries of the Divl. Arty. which could bring fire to bear on it fired 1 round gun fire with Shrapnel on it.	

2353 Wt. W2544/1454 700,000 5/15 D.D.&L. A.D.S.S./Forms/C. 2118.

Army Form C. 2118.

WAR DIARY
INTELLIGENCE SUMMARY
(Erase heading not required.)

Place	Date	Hour	Summary of Events and Information	Remarks and references to Appendices
BERTHONVAL	APRIL 29/15	P.M.	A minor operation was carried out this evening – The object was to take the craters opposite the left of P 79 – There are two craters opposite the end of BOYAU CENTRALE. The operation was unsuccessful, the craters were strongly held by the enemy with both men and machine guns.	
"	30"		2 Lieut. S. Page joined the Brigade on posting from the 25th D.A.C. He is posted to the R.A.C.	

H Boswell Lieut R.A
O/C 113 Bde R.A

25th. DIVISIONAL ARTILLERY

113th. BRIGADE R. F. A.

25th. DIVISIONAL ARTILLERY

MAY 1916.

WAR DIARY
or
INTELLIGENCE SUMMARY.
(Erase heading not required.)

Place	Date	Hour	Summary of Events and Information	Remarks and references to Appendices
BERTHONVAL FARM	MAY 1.		'C' Battery were heavily shelled with 5.9 in. Howitzers after tea this afternoon. No damage was done to the guns or the gun pits. Major F.B. KNYVETT who commands 'C' Battery was unfortunately wounded during the bombardment. He was sitting in his Mess (which is about 10 feet under ground) when a splinter came down the entrance and hit him just under the heart. He was taken to the nearest dressing station and he had the pieces of shell extracted and was back on duty at the Battery position again this evening.	
	3.		'C' Battery have erected wire screens in front of their guns in order to hide the flashes from the enemy observation balloons, which are always up. All this Batteries have been enlarging their gun pits to allow for a greater arc of fire. During the last few days 'C' Battery have come in for a lot of shelling. The German has also been paying much attention to the village of CARENCY.	

Army Form C. 2118.

WAR DIARY
~~INTELLIGENCE SUMMARY.~~
(Erase heading not required.)

Place	Date MAY	Hour	Summary of Events and Information	Remarks and references to Appendices
BERTHONVAL FM	3.	5 PM	Major KNYVETT has been hit again — This time in the back very near the spine. Very bad luck as the shell dropped some 100 yards or so away. He was walking behind his guns at the time. This time he will be to England, we expect.	
	4.		Situation quite normal during the morning. I sent MACSONNETH went up to 'C' Bty. This morning. He is in command of the Bty. now — Evening hate started about 5.30 PM. Some 5.9 again fell near 'C' Battery. About 7 PM 'D' Battery reported half the Essex Battery (Battery of 4 - 4.7" guns) were being shelled with 8 inch. This Battery is only about 200 yards behind 'D' Battery. At about 8 PM. 'A' Battery reported a small mine blown up about S 15 central. He occupied one side and the enemy the other.	
	5.		Situation at 4 AM was normal — Weather fine though rather more windy. The enemy started shelling — the light railway which runs up to the trenches just out taken at about 9 AM.	

HP

WAR DIARY
or
INTELLIGENCE SUMMARY
(Erase heading not required.)

Army Form C. 2118.

Place	Date MAY	Hour	Summary of Events and Information	Remarks and references to Appendices
BERTHONVAL FM	5		He kept it up all day. It got very overcast in the afternoon & this rendered observation difficult. A bombardment started about 8 PM. The London Division (47th) on our left started it. Enemy replied with shrapnel & beginning. The firing spread down to the front of the 74th Inf. Brigade (the left Brigade of our Division) It was reported that the enemy attacked at 9.90. Barrage fire was ordered. Only 'A' Battery fired. All was quiet again by 9 PM and our line reported intact.	
	6.	4.30 PM	Situation normal. Everything being quiet. It appears that there was no proper attack on P.90 last night. 'D' Battery report that the flashes of the 9.2" Hows: - who were firing a great deal last night - were very big. They are in action behind a wood, their flashes showed up the wood very clearly. Afternoon quite quiet. Weather overcast and much cooler. Observing Officer of 'A' Battery reports that there is a good deal of horse traffic on road running N. and S. behind German lines	

Army Form C. 2118.

WAR DIARY
or
INTELLIGENCE SUMMARY.
(Erase heading not required.)

Instructions regarding War Diaries and Intelligence Summaries are contained in F. S. Regs., Part II. and the Staff Manual respectively. Title pages will be prepared in manuscript.

Place	Date MAY	Hour	Summary of Events and Information	Remarks and references to Appendices
BÉRTHONVAL FM.	6		Moving N. into LENS. Time between 5 pm and 7 pm. The road is probably the main ARRAS-LENS road.	
	9	4.30 am	Situation normal. Everything very quiet all day (much rain and wind) until 7.45 pm when two mines were blown up by the enemy. One at about S 15 central & the other S 28 central. Great activity between 7.45 pm and 9.30 pm. 'A' Bty. fired 440 rounds and 'C' 142 during the day.	
	10	4.30 am	Situation normal.	
		12.20 pm	Requested by CRA to put 10 rounds opposite Q. 90 in retaliation	
		7.50	Orders to put 10 rounds opp. Q. 86. German Trench mortars active. The 7th In. Bde. asked for howitzer fire on craters at S 21 b 9530 .? Gave him 14 rounds which seemed to satisfy them. Ordered by CRA to register target by aeroplane. This was done by 'C' Battery at 3.30 pm. Quiet for rest of day.	

WAR DIARY
INTELLIGENCE SUMMARY

Army Form C. 2118.

Place	Date MAY	Hour	Summary of Events and Information	Remarks and references to Appendices
BERTHONVAL FM.	11	4.30 am	Situation normal. Infantry of 'P' Sector asked for support from howitzers over P 74 - 75 - 76. 'A' Battery fired six rounds which the Inf. considered enough. At 11.55 the enemy put five 5.9" shells into BERTHONVAL FARM - no damage done - Enemy fired about 250 5.9" shells into B/110 Bde Rd. between 3 pm and 6.30 pm. 'D' Battery fired 48 rounds on machine gun emplacements, knocked out one gun and damaged the emplacement of another. Otherwise all quiet.	
	12	4.30 am	Situation normal. At 10.45 Inf. of 'P' Sector asked for immediate retaliation opposite P 79. 'C' Battery gave them 30 rounds at 2 rounds per minute. Allowance of ammunition to be dumped with each gun raised to 250.	
	13.	4.30 am	Situation normal. Very quiet all day. Rain raised. Counter Batteries requested to fire 4 rounds at 8 pm.	J.P.

Army Form C. 2118.

WAR DIARY
or
INTELLIGENCE SUMMARY
(Erase heading not required.)

Instructions regarding War Diaries and Intelligence Summaries are contained in F. S. Regs., Part II. and the Staff Manual respectively. Title pages will be prepared in manuscript.

Place	Date MAY	Hour	Summary of Events and Information	Remarks and references to Appendices
BERTRONVAL FM	14	4.30 am	Situation normal. Orders came in re. abolition of R.A.C. and re-organisation of A.A.C. also new arrangement of Howitzer Brigades. Trouble with H.Q. CRA about receipt for bivouacs etc. handed over to 46 K Division. 'A' Battery gave receipt to R.A.C. for 330 rounds of ammunition which has never been received – result, much hostile in the office and the return was late. All quiet to rest of day on our front, but heavy firing on left of London Division.	
	15		At 6.30 am orders came from CRA that 'A' Battery would be under the orders of O.C. 112 Bde. for the rest of the day. Small operation to come off in the evening. Quiet all day as far as we were concerned. At 8.30. a minor operation was carried out in front of Q. 89. q.1. 'A' Battery was placed under O.C 112 Bde. 'C' Battery was called upon to fire on right lines with good result. Report that operation was a success has come in.	

WAR DIARY
INTELLIGENCE SUMMARY

Place	Date	Hour	Summary of Events and Information	Remarks and references to Appendices
B-VAH FM.	MAY 16		Things were quiet all day with our Batteries. Though the enemy fired a large number of shells at different points. 'A' Btty. was placed under the command of G.O.C. 74th Inf. Brigade and we were called upon to put down a direct line from 'A' Bty. to Brigade HQ. This order did not come in until 6.45 PM, men did not finish until 6.30 AM the 17th inst.	
	17.		Nothing much doing. During the last 7 days C/113 have had to renovate their O.P. twice owing to it being knocked about by shell fire.	
	18.		Relief Orders came in this morning. The 47th Division is extending its front Southwards and taking over Sector 'Q' of the 25th Div. front. The 51st Division is extending its front northwards and taking over Sectors 'O' and 'P'. The relief of the Artillery is taking place on the following nights 19/20, 20/21, 21/22.	HP.

Army Form C. 2118.

WAR DIARY
or
INTELLIGENCE SUMMARY.
(Erase heading not required.)

Place	Date MAY	Hour	Summary of Events and Information	Remarks and references to Appendices
B--VAL FM.	18		We are handing over stripped guns to the incoming unit. This does not apply to 'A' Battery as no one is going into their position.- One section of 'D' Battery and C/113 are being relieved on the night of 19/20 by D/255 and D/255 respectively. They each take over, on coming out, two howitzers at the 31st Div. Batteries at PREVIN-CAPELLE. The relief of the remaining two sections takes place on the 21/22. On the same night 'A' Battery withdraw to their wagon lines.	
		10 PM	The Germans attacked our post on Crater P.79/1 and captured it. Our counter attacks was unsuccessful.	
	19		One section of 'C' Battery and one section of 'D' Battery relieved to-night. Relief completed by 9 PM (about).	
		9.15 PM	Crater P. 79/1 was successfully attacked and recaptured.	

Army Form C. 2118.

WAR DIARY
or
INTELLIGENCE SUMMARY.
(Erase heading not required.)

Instructions regarding War Diaries and Intelligence Summaries are contained in F.S. Regs., Part II. and the Staff Manual respectively. Title pages will be prepared in manuscript.

Place	Date MAY	Hour	Summary of Events and Information	Remarks and references to Appendices
B-VAL FM.	20.		Nothing to report. On being relieved the Brigade will go back into the Rest Area - to GRAND CAMP where we were before. A billeting (Advance) Party is going on to GRAND CAMP to-morrow morning.	
	21.		At about 5 AM the enemy heavily bombarded the left of 'P' Sector, he kept it up until about 10 AM. At 3.30 PM the enemy opened a very heavy bombardment on the front of 'P' and 'Q' Sectors. The bombardment has been very well organised, everything and everybody is attended to - all the light railways and tracks leading to the front line are being very heavily shelled, chiefly with tear shells. The batteries of the 110th Brigade and our own 'C' Battery are getting a great number of tear shells. The relief of the remaining section of D/113 is being cancelled. Remaining section of C/113 in front of 'O' Sector.	

WAR DIARY
or
INTELLIGENCE SUMMARY.
(Erase heading not required.)

Place	Date MAY	Hour	Summary of Events and Information	Remarks and references to Appendices
B--VAL FM	21.		The relief of 'A' Battery has also been cancelled – Brigade Headquarters are not moving back either. The Colonel and myself (Adjutant) with Six telephonists are staying. The remaining telephonists and officers Servants etc. are returning to the wagon line. At about 10 PM the enemy made an attack against the Right of 'Q' Sector and the junction of 'P' and 'Q' Sectors. This afternoon Major CAREW-HUNT, Comdg. D/113, was ordered to Command and take into action to-night a Composite Battery made up of the Section of C/113 and the Section of D/113 relieved on the 19/20. The Battery was taken into action near VILLERS AU BOIS X 13 d 30. The range to the German front line was about 6000 yards. During the evening the Germans put a great many tear shell in front of the FARM and	

WAR DIARY
or
INTELLIGENCE SUMMARY

(Erase heading not required.)

Place	Date MAY	Hour	Summary of Events and Information	Remarks and references to Appendices
B--VAL PM.	21		up and down the light railway. The Tel Shell are very obsternate and make it very awkward for reading and writing messages and telephoning. At about 10 PM the enemy attacked the right of 'Q' Sector and the left of 'P' Sector. Cannot get much information back from the Infantry. It appears that our front line and support trenches have been captured. No casualties in the Brigade.	
	22		Still a good deal of shelling during the morning. One of the howitzers belonging to the section of 'D' Battery which was relieved last night has to be taken into action at LA TARGETTE (just behind NEUVILLE ST VAAST) 2/Lieut. ALSTON is detailed to do this. The Colonel reconnoitred the position. The howitzer was taken up about 9 PM. Position is very exposed; being only 1500x (about) from the front trenches and under machine gun fire. Brigade H.Q. got orders in the afternoon to move back to the Wagon Line at CAPELLE-FERMONT.	

WAR DIARY
INTELLIGENCE SUMMARY
(Erase heading not required.)

Army Form C. 2118.

Place	Date MAY	Hour	Summary of Events and Information	Remarks and references to Appendices
B---VAL FM	22		We were all clear of the FARM by 9.30 PM. 'C' Bty are under the 110th Brigade and 'A' Bty. under the 112th Bde.	
CARELLE FERMONT	23.		2/Lt. ALSTON got the howitzer into position at LA TARGETTE without any hindrance. Two wagon loads of ammunition (108 rounds) have been dumped with the gun. 2/Lt. Alston is under the direct orders of C.R.A. Lt. BRITTAIN, D/113, is going to relieve 2/Lt. Alston – this evening – We are going to make a counter-attack this evening.	
	24.		Lt Schooling and 2/Lt Jennings got back from St. MICHEL at 9 A.M. They went there on the 21st with the Advance Party. Our counter-attack last night unsuccessful. One of 'A' Battery's howitzers out of action – Due to a premature (elevating gear) Bringing it down to the Wagon Line tonight. 'A' Battery's orderly killed in CARENCY.	

HP.

WAR DIARY
or
INTELLIGENCE SUMMARY.
(Erase heading not required.)

Army Form C. 2118.

Place	Date MAY	Hour	Summary of Events and Information	Remarks and references to Appendices
CAPELLE FERMONT	25		Orders received that 'A' Batty. will withdraw to their wagon Line to-night at 9 P.M. Composite Battery under Major Cakes - Hunt withdrawing to wagon Line also - withdrawal of 'A' Battery to the wagon Line cancelled.	
		10 PM	Composite Battery arrived at wagon line -	
	26		One of the howitzers of the Composite Battery had to be sent in to the I.O.M. at SAVY this morning - A premature had stripped the lands for a distance of 3 or 4 in. near the muzzle. Orders recd. for Brigade HQ, 'C' Battery (1 Section) and 'D' Battery to go into their old positions again this evening. 'A' Battery are to withdraw to their wagon line leaving the gun position at 9 P.M. Lt. GATES, A/113, is relieving Lt. Britain at LATTRGETTE his evening at 9 PM. 200 rounds are now kept dumped with this howitzer. Left CAPELLE - FERMONT at 6 PM. All moves and reliefs carried out successfully -	

WAR DIARY or INTELLIGENCE SUMMARY

Army Form C. 2118.

Place	Date	Hour	Summary of Events and Information	Remarks and references to Appendices
BERTHONVAL FM.	MAY 27.		Lieut Brittain, D/113, is taking over the howitzer at La Targette again this evening. One section of 'A' Battery are coming into action in a new position in a sunken road about 500 to 600 yards S.W. of Berthonval Farm to-night. They are slinging up 1 gun to-take then, the second they are getting from 'D' Battery's position to-night. (D/113 will then have 3 guns at their Battery position only) the odd one being at La Targette). The re-organization of the D.A.C. is now taking place - All the R.A.C's are being broken up. Capt. Sheat, O.C. 113 R.A.C. is on leave at present - another officer in the R.A.C, 2Lieut Page is attending an Artillery Course at the Third Army Artillery School - Lieut Schooling is therefore doing the duties of O.C R.A.C. The 113th Brigade will shortly be split up - It has been decided	AP

WAR DIARY
or
INTELLIGENCE SUMMARY.
(Erase heading not required.)

Place	Date MAY	Hour	Summary of Events and Information	Remarks and references to Appendices
B-VAL FM	27		that the Howitzer Batteries of a Division shall no longer be grouped together and form a How: Brigade. A Howitzer Bty is going to be attached to each 18-Pdr. Brigade. The three old 18-Pdr Batteries thus displaced will form an 18-Pdr Brigade under the old Headquarters of the How: Bde. This will involve the changing of the numbers of Batteries. Our present 'A' Battery will go to the 110th Brigade and become D/110. The present D/110 will then become A/113 and come to this Brigade. Our 'C' Battery will become D/111 - D/111 will become B/113 - 'D' Battery will become D/112 - D/112 will become C/113 - This change will not take place until we go back to the Reserve Area.	
	28		'A' Battery have to move their wagon line from CAMBLAIN to CAPELLE - FERMONT to-day - The two howitzers which	

WAR DIARY or INTELLIGENCE SUMMARY

Army Form C. 2118.

Place	Date MAY	Hour	Summary of Events and Information	Remarks and references to Appendices
B--VAL Fm	28		had to go go to the I.O.M. at Pavy for repair have been returned - 'A' Battery have taken them both - 'A' Bty are bringing up their remaining two guns into position to-night. They are not to fire without special orders from C.R.A. owing to the fact that they are very near the road up which all the infantry supplies etc. come every night.	
	29		The re-organisation of the N.A.C. has been completed to-day - 'C' Battery have been put under the tactical command of the 110th and 'D' Bty under the 111th. Not much point in our staying up here!	
	30		Brigade Headquarters and 'A' Battery are withdrawing to the Wagon Line to-night - Lt.-Col. SELIGMAN Comdg. 257 Brigade is taking over from us. We left for the Wagon Line at about 9 PM - 'C' Bty and 'D' Bty are not being relieved yet, but are staying in action and have come under Col. Seligman.	4.

Army Form C. 2118.

WAR DIARY
INTELLIGENCE SUMMARY.
(Erase heading not required.)

Place	Date MAY	Hour	Summary of Events and Information	Remarks and references to Appendices
CAPELLE FERMONT	31.		The Colonel and Lieut. Scholing went on to ST. MICHEL at 8 AM this morning. 'A' Battery and Brigade Headquarters march at 9 PM. 'A' Battery march out as A/113 but when they get to St. Michel they join the 110th Brigade and become D/110. The present D/110 and D/111 march to-night and join the 113 Brigade at St. Michel and become A/113 and B/113. The present D/112 is already at St. Michel and will become C/113.	Hornall LTRA Col 113 Bde RA
		4 PM	Orders received from the CRA in person that the following Batteries are going to remain in their wagon lines for the present under the orders of the Colonel. (Lt. Col. F. F. LAMBARDE) ½ A/110, ½ C/110, B/110, D/110 (which becomes A/113 after midnight) A/111, ½ B/111, ½ C/111, D/111 (B/113 after midnight) = A/113 (D/110 after midnight) will proceed to GRAND CAMP as previously ordered. CRa. is sending his car to St. Michel to bring back the Colonel.	

2353. Wt. W2511/1454 700,000 5/15 D, D. & L. A.D.S.S./Forms/C. 2118.

Army Form C. 2118.

WAR DIARY
or
INTELLIGENCE SUMMARY.
(Erase heading not required.)

Place	Date	Hour	Summary of Events and Information	Remarks and references to Appendices
			ADDENDA	
			Lieut. N.S. MACDONNELL was promoted to the rank of Temp. Captain whilst in command of 'C' Battery, vice Major F.B. KNYVETT wounded.	
			Lieut. A.C.R. DAVID was transferred from the B.A.C. to the D.A.C. with effect from 28.2.5.16	
			The undermentioned officers were promoted 1st Lieutenants with effect from 28.4.16	
			2/Lieuts. A.P. EVERSHED ⎫ L. MACEWAN ⎬ A/113 I.J.L. HOLLINGTON ⎭	
			C. KENNEDY ⎫ E.S. BRITTAIN ⎬ D/113	
			H. SOMERVILLE-SMITH C/113	
			A.C.R. DAVID . B.A.C.	

25th. DIVISIONAL ARTILLERY

113th. BRIGADE R. F. A.

25th. DIVISIONAL ARTILLERY

J U N E   1 9 1 6.

J/39

Officer i/c A.G's Office at the Base.

Enclosed please find
War diary. 113 Brigade
R.F.A. for the month of
June 1916.

6/7/16

.... Col. R.F.A.
Comd'g 113th Brigade R.F.A.

WAR DIARY
or
INTELLIGENCE SUMMARY.
(Erase heading not required.)

Army Form C. 2118.

113 BRIGADE R.F.A.
25 DIVISION
JUNE
Vol 8

Place	Date	Hour	Summary of Events and Information	Remarks and references to Appendices
CAPELLE FERMONT	1		The Section of C/110 is marching back to the Reserve Area to-night and the Section of A/110 (already in the Reserve Area) is marching to CAPELLE - FERMONT to-night. This will complete A/110. B/111 are being completed in the same way to-night. All six batteries are being attached to the 51st Division. A/110 goes into action on night 2/3. Position: One section at A 26 a 37. One section at A 26 c 0085. B/110 going into action to-night into their old position. A/111 going up into action to-night into their old position. B/111 goes into action to-morrow night the 2/3 at F 18 c 66. A/113 (the old D/110) will go into action on the night of the 2/3 at G 2 c 7510. B/113 going into action to-night into their old position. Orders received later that A/110 not going into action until the night 3/4.	Reference Maps 36ᶜ 36ᵇ 51ᶜ 51ᵇ N.W. 1/40,000

WAR DIARY or INTELLIGENCE SUMMARY.

(Erase heading not required.)

JUNE

Army Form C. 2118.

Place	Date	Hour	Summary of Events and Information	Remarks and references to Appendices
CAPELLE FERMONT	2		All moves carried out in accordance with orders last night. Brigade Headquarters are moving back to ST. MICHEL to-night. We are not going back to the woods in GRANDCAMP, but are going under canvas quite close by, within ½ mile. Left about 6 PM to ST. MICHEL. Veterinary Officer is staying behind.	
ST. MICHEL	3 & 6 & 6		The camp is quite nice, soon gets very muddy when there is a little rain. Only C/113 here of course; A/113 - B/113 up in the line in action. We have a Heavy Trench Mortar Battery to look after now. This Battery forms part of the Brigade - The Battery is commanded by Lieut. P. CHAWORTH-MUSTERS R.F.A. On the 7/5 2Lieut KIRKHAM and 66 other ranks of W/25 Heavy Trench Mortar Battery proceeded to ECOIVRES in motor lorries. They are attached to the XVII Corps. The weather is not very good. We have here "Divisional Schemes every other day. A large tract of country has been purchased for training purposes.	

WAR DIARY or INTELLIGENCE SUMMARY.

Army Form C. 2118.

JUNE

Place	Date	Hour	Summary of Events and Information	Remarks and references to Appendices
ST. MICHEL	11		Great Scheme of communications just issued by Division - This Scheme is worked out for the time when we advance. Brigade Headquarters, working under this new System, will require 24 Signallers.	Ref. MAP LENS 1/100,000
	12.		Field day coming off to-morrow the 13th inst - There has been a rehearsal to-day - The Colonel, Jennings and myself placed ourselves as enemy observation officers and reported on the visibility of our infantry etc.	
	13		Very bad day - Scheme went off alright all right - 'C' Battery were attached to the 110th Brigade for the Scheme, so that 113 Bde - HQ. having no batteries to command, had nothing to do and did nothing. Orders in for the move to OUTREBOIS - We move on Thursday, 15th.	

Note OUTREBOIS is about 4-5 miles N.W. of DOULLENS

WAR DIARY
or
INTELLIGENCE SUMMARY.
(Erase heading not required.)

Army Form C. 2118.

JUNE

Place	Date	Hour	Summary of Events and Information	Remarks and references to Appendices
ST. MICHEL	14		Advance Party for the Brigade left for OUTREBOIS at 4 AM. The Brigade (less A/113 and B/113) move off at 9.45 AM to-morrow morning. Twice advanced 60 minutes to-day; 11 PM became 12 midnight.	
	15		Quite a nice day - we moved out of camp at about 9.15 AM. We had a very slow march, great deal of traffic on the roads. FREVENT was very congested. Arrived eventually about 6 PM. Nine hours on the road and the distance was only about 16 miles =	
OUTREBOIS	16		Lovely day. Orders received that the 113 Brigade is going to be attached to the French Army - A/113 and B/113 were relieved last night > 15/16, by two batteries of the 38th Division - They rejoin us to-day - we march to VILLERS BOCAGE to-morrow - Further orders will then be issued by Fourth Army =	Ref. Maps LENS & AMIENS 1/100,000 VILLERS BOCAGE is 7-8 miles N. of AMIENS
		12 midnight	No sign of 'A' and 'B' Batteries =	
	17		A/113 arrived at about 5.15 AM after marching all night. They have got no rations or forage for to-day; their supply wagons have been lost temporally. No sign of	

WAR DIARY
or
INTELLIGENCE SUMMARY.

TONE

Place	Date	Hour	Summary of Events and Information	Remarks and references to Appendices
OUTREBOIS	17		'B' Battery yet. We have got a new C.R.A. General BETHELL has gone to England. New C.R.A. is Gen. KIRMAN. Heard that Advance Party of 'B' Battery is at BARLEY. B Battery arrived here at about 2.15 PM. B/143 Brigade HQ. A/143 - C/143 marched off at 3 PM - B/143 halted at BARLY for 2 hours, moved off again at 4.15 PM. Move of the Brigade to VILLERS BOCAGE completed by 11.30 PM. Orders received; the Brigade with we transferred to the Groupe d'Armées du Nord. Brigade to be prepared to entrain to - morrow afternoon in neighbourhood of AMIENS. Destination, PIERREFONDS, S.E. of COMPIEGNE where we shall be under the orders of the X French Army. 64th Brigade R.F.A. of the 12th Division are also being attached to X French Army.	
VILLERS BOCAGE	18.		Supplies have dumped 4 days rations and forage for us. This is up to and including the 22nd. It took 2 motor lorries (3-ton lorries) to bring it - they have given us 4 G.S. wagons to take it away - Nothing more about entraining.	

Army Form C. 2118.

WAR DIARY
or
INTELLIGENCE SUMMARY
(Erase heading not required.)

JUNE

Place	Date	Hour	Summary of Events and Information	Remarks and references to Appendices
VILLERS BOCAGE	18	9 PM	Orders received - First train - Brigade HQ - A/113 - ½ B/113 - entrain at 3 PM to-morrow at LONGUEAU - Second train - C/113 - ½ B/113 - entrain at 6 PM.	LONGUEAU is 2-3 miles S.E. of AMIENS
	19		Bde. HQ - A/113 - ½ B/113 moved off at 10 AM. C/113 - ½ B/113 moved at 1 PM. Distance to station about 12 miles. First train moved out of LONGUEAU at 6.30 PM, Second train, under Capt. BARKER. O.C. C/113, at 9.30 PM.	
VENETTE	20		First train arrived at RETHONDES at 12.30 AM. Second train at 4 AM. The Brigade marched at 7 AM and reached VENETTE (about 1 kilometre from COMPIEGNE) at 9 AM. No billets etc ready for us, 64 Brigade R.3.A. arrived here last night.	
	21		We are attached to the 26 Division, 13th Army Corps. Reconnaissance of Battery positions etc. this morning by Colonel - Adjutant - Signalling Officer Battery Commanders and 1 Subaltern per Battery. Brigade HQ. will be at ST. LEGER - All three Batteries together at TAILLEPIED, only 1600x from ST. LEGER. Decided to move from VENETTE to PLESSIS BRION - lie evening. Brigade marched out of VENETTE at 5 PM- arrived PLESSIS BRION at about 6.30 PM. Horse lines in the wood, men at in the wood also. Brigade HQ. in the Chateau, very comfortable.	

WAR DIARY
INTELLIGENCE SUMMARY

Army Form C. 2118.

JUNE

Place	Date	Hour	Summary of Events and Information	Remarks and references to Appendices
PLESSIS BRION	22		Lovely day, very hot. We are relieving, at TAILLEPIED, three Batteries of 75's belonging to the 16th Regiment of Artillery. One gun per Battery taken up into action to-day to purpose of registration. Each Battery is sending up 3 Telephonists to morrow. 64th Brigade arrived here late last night. Congestion with two Brigades in the village is rather bad. Watering of horses is going to be difficult. It is forbidden to use the River (l'OISE) which runs within 400x of the horse lines, as it is impossible to water there without being under observation of German balloons. We have to use the wells in the village.	
	23		Orders were received in the afternoon that we should complete the relief of the French Batteries to morrow 24th between 2 PM and 5 PM. Quite possible to effect the relief at this time because the batteries are in the edge of a wood which extends right down to PLESSIS BRION. Orders re. relief cancelled and date altered to 25th.	
	24		We are getting all our telephones installed to-day. Very difficult business. The French use a ringing 'phone so we cannot use our D III in conjunction with their instrument. All communications were fixed up by 6 PM. for the purpose of liaison, Frenchmen speaking English are being attached to us as follows: Battalion HQ. 2 men. Each Battery 1 man	HP

Army Form C. 2118.

WAR DIARY
or
INTELLIGENCE SUMMARY.
(Erase heading not required.)

JUNE

Place	Date	Hour	Summary of Events and Information	Remarks and references to Appendices
PLESSIS BRION	24		Brigade HQ 2 men. Remaining three guns per Battery going into action to morrow morning. Relief is to be completed by 9 AM. Brigade HQ. moving up to ST. LEGER to-morrow morning; we take over the command as soon as the Relief is complete. Wagon Lines staying at PLESSIS BRION.	
ST. LEGER	25		Relief was completed by 3.15 AM. Everything went off quite satisfactorily satisfactorily. One French officer per Battery is staying behind with our Batteries for a day or two, who they get settled down. Captain Roux, who commanded the 16th Regiment is staying with Brigade HQ. for a day or two also.	
	27		Very quiet all yesterday. General Commanding the Corps Artillery inspected our Batteries and Wagon Lines - Very pleased with all he saw. Bombardment started on the left of our zone - PIMPREZ - about 10 PM. Fire slackened down at 11 PM - Started again at 1 AM, all quiet at 1.30 AM. Brigade fired 300 rounds in all. Between 10 PM and 11 PM "C" Battery were heavily shelled with 5.9" Howitzers. (about 100-150 shells) No casualties to men or material.	
	28		Very quiet day. The 26th Division is being relieved by the 81st Division. General Commanding the 81st Division went round our Batteries in the afternoon.	HP

War Diary.

D.T.L./V.S.

Place	Date	Hour	Summary of Events and Information.
			JUNE
ST. LEGER	30		Very quiet yesterday. The Infantry of the 26th Division are being relieved to-night. The Infantry of the 81st Division are Territorials. They are all men of about 40 years of age. At 10.15 PM a German aeroplane dropped 2 bombs just N. of the Batteries of the 64th Brigade which are at ST. HUBERT. Note ST. HUBERT is about 1 km. W. of ST. LEGER.
			Attached
			Nominal roll of officers of the 113 Brigade R.F.A.

J Howarth Lieut RFA
Adjt 113 Brigade RFA

NOMINAL ROLL OF OFFICERS OF THE 113TH BRIGADE R.F.A.

Brigade Headquarters.

Lieut. Col. F.F. Lambarde, D.S.O.
Lieut. F.H.S. Pownall, Adjutant.
Lieut. J. Schooling, Orderly Officer.
2/Lieut. F.N. Jennings, Signalling Officer.

"A" Battery.

Captain R.G. Purcell.
Lieut. F.F. Meadows.
Lieut. J.F. Parker.
2/Lieut. S.W. Harris.
2/Lieut. T.D. Lane.

"B" Battery.

Major D.W. Osborne.
2/ Lieut. G.W. Biggs.
Lieut. W. Miller.
2/Lieut. W. Horsfield.
2/Lieut. W. Aitchison.

"C" Battery.

Captain A. Barker.
Lieut. D. Ive.
Lieut. D.L. Jones.
2/Lieut. F.D. Swinford.

Attached.

Captain H.W. Binks, R.A.M.C.
Captain J.J. Farrell, A.V.C.

Pownall Lieut. R.F.A.
Adjutant 113th Brigade R.F.A.

25th Div.

WAR DIARY

Headquarters,

113th BRIGADE, R.F.A.

J U L Y

1 9 1 5

INTELLIGENCE SUMMARY

113 Brigade R.F.A.

Vol 9 July

Summary of Events and Information	Remarks and references to Appendices
heavily shelled.	
...nated to the Hospital in COMPIEGNE.	
...cers joined the Brigade from the R.M.A.	
...osted to A/113	
" " C/113	
the front of the Division on our left. Registering (O.P.)	
3 granted a commission and posted to ...oceeded to Railhead 30th June, to-day ...manding the Artillery of the Third Army (FRENCH)	
Promoted to TEMP. LIEUT. with effect from 20 May 1916	H.

To Headquarters
25th Division Artillery

Herewith War Diary of 113th Bde R.F.A. which was not forwarded with other diaries of Div'l Artillery, owing to this Bde being with French army

DWhyndaCapt
for
Brig.-Genl.
Commanding 25th Div. Arty.

4.8.16

J Lawrence
Comd'g 113th Brigade R.F.A.
Col. R.F.A.

INTELLIGENCE SUMMARY.

113 Brigade R.F.A.

July Vol 9

(Erase heading not required.)

Date	Summary of Events and Information	Remarks and references to Appendices
	Staff Capt. 25/7/16	
	Herewith Diary for the month of July.	
	H. Pownall Lieut: R.F.A. ADJUTANT 113th BRIGADE R.F.A.	
	heavily shelled.	
	evacuated to the hospital in COMPIEGNE.	
	...cers joined the Brigade from the R.M.A.	
	posted to A/113	
	" " C/113	
	...the front of the Division on our left. Registering (O.P.)	
	...3 granted a commission and posted to ...oceeded to Railhead 30th Divn: 15-day ...manding the Artillery of the Third Army (FRENCH)	
30.7.16	...omoted to TEMP. LIEUT. with effect from 20. May 1916	H.P.

J. Lawrence
Comdg 113th Brigade R.F.A.
Col. R.F.A.

INTELLIGENCE SUMMARY.

(Erase heading not required.)

113 Brigade R.F.A.

Vol 9 July

Staff Manual respectively. Title pages and ... will be prepared in manuscript.

Place	Date	Hour	Summary of Events and Information	Remarks and references to Appendices
ST. LEGER	1st		Balcon (Observation Station) heavily shelled.	
	8th		2 Lieut. LANE, A/113, evacuated to the Hospital in COMPIEGNE.	
			The undermentioned Officers joined the Brigade from the R.M.A.	
			2 Lieut J.W. STOBART, posted to A/113	
			2 Lieut D.R. MACNEIL, " " C/113	
	9th		Batteries registered on the front of the Division on our left. Registering was done from ANTOVAL. (O.P.)	
	10th		B.S.M. BATEMAN of C/113 granted a commission and posted to 30th Divisional Arty. Proceeded to Railhead 30th Divn. to-day.	
	20th		General MOJON, commanding the Artillery of the Third Army (FRENCH) inspected the Batteries.	
	26th		2 Lieut F.D. SWINFORD promoted to TEMP. LIEUT. with effect from 20. May 1916.	H.

J Lawranson
Col. R.F.A.
Comdg 113th Brigade R.F.A.

25th Divisional Artillery

113th BRIGADE

ROYAL FIELD ARTILLERY

AUGUST 1 9 1 6

Army Form C. 2118.

WAR DIARY
or
INTELLIGENCE SUMMARY.
(Erase heading not required.)

113th Brigade R.F.A. Vol 10

AUGUST

Instructions regarding War Diaries and Intelligence Summaries are contained in F. S. Regs., Part II. and the Staff Manual respectively. Title pages will be prepared in manuscript.

Place	Date	Hour	Summary of Events and Information	Remarks and references to Appendices
ST LEGER	1st		The Brigade is still with the 64th Brigade R.F.A., attached to the 8th Division of the French Army, which covers the area CANAL DE L'OISE — TRACY LEVAL — PUISALEINE. All the Batteries of the Brigade are in action at TAILLEFIED with waggon lines at LE PLESSIS BRION. Head Quarters of the Brigade are at ST LEGER AUX BOIS also the Hd Qrs of 162 Infantry Brigade (French), the Western Sector of whose front the Brigade covers. 43 rounds fired on enemy's working parties near PIMPREZ at request of Infantry.	
	2nd		64th Brigade R.F.A. detached and sent to join the 87th Division.	
	4th		The Brigade was officially photographed for Records of the French Army.	
	5th		199 fired at request of O.C. Divisional Arty and Infantry at Machine Gun emplacements in BAILLY, BRIDGES at PIMPREZ, and in retaliation of enemy's Trench Mortar fire. Our Batteries shelled by enemy with 105 c.m. shells. No Casualties.	
	6th		13 rounds fired on Machine guns, BAILLY, at request of Infantry	

Army Form C. 2118.

WAR DIARY
or
INTELLIGENCE SUMMARY.
(Erase heading not required.)

AUGUST.

Instructions regarding War Diaries and Intelligence Summaries are contained in F. S. Regs., Part II. and the Staff Manual respectively. Title pages will be prepared in manuscript.

Place	Date	Hour	Summary of Events and Information	Remarks and references to Appendices
ST LEGER.	7.		30 Rounds fired on Machine Gun emplacements, BAILLY, at request of Infantry.	
	8.		56 Rounds fired on and near BAILLY at request of Infantry.	
	9.		50 rounds fired on Machine Gun emplacements, BAILLY.	
	10.		No firing.	
	11.		About 30 rounds were fired on working party near BAILLY.	
	12.		100 rounds expended in Registration and fire on Machine gun on ext. regiment of Infantry.	
	13.		24 rounds expended on Working Parties.	
	14.		42 rounds expended on Working parties etc.	
	15.		17 rounds fired on the MAISON NOIRE and Machine Gun emplacement in BAILLY. Infantry reporting that work was being carried out there. 6 Bombs dropped round Observation Post, BALCON. No casualties.	
	16.		Nothing special to report.	
	17.		32 rounds between 10 p.m. and 11 p.m. on transport and working parties reported by the Infantry.	
	18.		Nothing to report.	

WAR DIARY or INTELLIGENCE SUMMARY

Army Form C. 2118.

AUGUST.

Place	Date	Hour	Summary of Events and Information	Remarks and references to Appendices
ST LEGER.	19th		Nothing to report.	
	20th		26 rounds expended on working party.	
	21st		41 rounds on working party and Machine Gun emplacement. Annual Musketry Examination 43/66 qualified for "Flag".	
	22nd		20 rounds fired at the regiment of Infantry.	
	23rd		At midday the Infantry called for fire on point 6208. 7005 were again fired on demand from Infantry – 24 rounds fired.	
	24th	3am.	14 rounds Shrapnel fired on M.G. line.	
	25th		Quiet on our front.	
	26th		17 Rounds H.E. fired at:- Machine gun emplacement in BAILLY (+512) Left regiment of Infantry. 30 rounds Shrapnel fired into TRANCHÉES de BAILLY (6609) at 9am. & 12.30pm.	
	27th	12.15	24 rounds Shrapnel on MAISON NOIRE (6607) 50 rounds expended on other points – retaliation for enemy fire on BAILLY.	
	28th		Observation Post at BALCON shelled by enemy's 5.9".	
	29th		120 rounds fired on various points in retaliation etc.	

Army Form C. 2118.

WAR DIARY
or
INTELLIGENCE SUMMARY.

(Erase heading not required.)

AUGUST

Place	Date	Hour	Summary of Events and Information	Remarks and references to Appendices
ST LEGER	30th		50 rounds expended on various points in retaliation.	
	31st		200 rounds fired in retaliation &c.	

Saunders Lt. Col. R.F.A.
Comd'g 118th Brigade R.F.A.
31/8/16

13° Corps d'Armée   B O I S des R I G O L E S

Secteur Ouest   (ou Bois Carré)

Artillerie

I°.- **RENSEIGNEMENTS GENERAUX**.-

        Les C.P. d'Infanterie signalent assez fréquemment des bruits de travaux dans le Bois Carré. Le 3 Août, de nouveaux réseaux de fil de fer sont signalés devant le Bois des Rigoles.
        Les photos récentes donnent peu de renseignements en raison de la végétation.

2°.- **OBJECTIFS PARTICULIERS**.-

    Mitrailleuses.- Deux emplacements certains :
        I°.- 5906 - près de la corne Sud du Bois carré.
        2°.- entre 60.07 et 61.08 - tire le 7 Août sur nos premières lignes et le I2 Août contre avion, tirant également les 24 et 25 Août.

    Observatoires.- Le 5 Août, un appareil mobile paraissant être un périscope est vu en face du Moulin de Bailly.
    Les 6 Août (7 et 9), deux périscopes signalés en 60.07 et 61.08.

    Postes de tireurs.- Dans la nuit du 3I Juillet au Ier Août, des tireurs occupent les arbres vers la corne S et tirent dans nos tranchées.

    Abris.- Deux zônes d'abris.
        Abris de première ligne vers la corne S du bois et en arrière de la lisière S.E.
        Abris de deuxième ligne (point moyen 60.I0) vers la corne N. pour réserves.
        Les tirs exécutés jusqu'ici n'ont atteint que les premiers.

    Pistes.- - de la forêt d'Ourscamp à la corne N. du Bois Carré.
        - de la lisière E et de la corne S.E. allant vers l'Oise.

(Photo C.I0
A.590) du
I4/4/I6

    Noeuds de boyaux importants.- (1) $\begin{cases} x = 46.050 \\ y = 50I.I20 \end{cases}$ (2) $\begin{cases} x = 46.I00 \\ y = 50I.050 \end{cases}$

    (I) - arrivée du gros boyau venant de la Forêt d'Ourscamp (utilisé pour relève & ravitaillement).
    (2) - noeud de boyau présentant en outre un gros ouvrage.

                      P.C. le 28 Août 1916.
                      Le Lt-Colonel d'ALAYER Cdt l'A.S.C.

I3° Corps d'Armée   T I R

Secteur Ouest   SUR LE BOIS DES RIGOLES.

Artillerie

N° S/40

BUT DU TIR.- Destruction des mitrailleuses, observatoires et abris organisés dans le Bois des Rigoles.

DIRECTEUR DU TIR.- ~~Lt-Colonel LAMPARDE~~ Major Willoughby-Osbourne, Cdt la II3ème Brigade R.F.A.

BATTERIES PRENANT PART A L'ACTION.- 3 Bies de 85 — II3° Bde R.F.A.
- A Capitaine PURCELL
- B Capitaine ~~WILLOUGHBY~~
- C Capitaine BARKER

REPARTITION DE L'OBJECTIF.- Chaque batterie bat la zône qui lui est désignée par le croquis ci-joint, elle répartit l'intensité de ses feux de façon à agir principalement sur l'objectif défini qui lui est assigné dans l'intérieur de sa zône.

Unités	Zône d'action	Objectifs principaux	Dépense prévue
Bie ~~B~~	Partie S.O. 5807-5906-6007-5908	Mitrailleuse 5906 abris, noeuds de boyaux	400 A.X. 60 A ~~200 Coups~~
Bie ~~A~~	Partie du Centre 5908-6007-6I08-60I0	Mitrailleuse 6I08 Noeuds de boyaux	500 A.X. 60 A ~~200 Coups~~
Bie C	Partie Nord 60I0-6I08-60I0-60II	Noeuds de boyaux 60II-6II0 Abris	400 A.X. 60 A ~~200 Coups~~

CONDUITE DU TIR.- Deux phases :

I°.- Tir d'efficacité — ~~Les batteries agiront simultanément à l'heure H de façon à produire, autant que possible, un effet de surprise.~~

2°.- Tir de harcèlement.- Pendant les deux nuits qui suivent le tir d'efficacité, la batterie B tirera plusieurs salves à intervalles irréguliers, pour gêner les travaux de réparations.   20 A.

La dépense de munitions indiquée ci-dessus est pour les deux tirs.

TIRS de REGLAGES.- Les réglages seront effectués la veille du jour fixé pour les tirs, ou dans la matinée du jour du tir.

25th DIVISION
ARTILLERY.

113th. BRIGADE R. F. A.

25th. DIVISIONAL ARTILLERY

SEPTEMBER 1 9 1 6.

P. 53

Staff Capt 25 D.A.

Herewith please find enclosed War Diary for this Brigade for the month of September 1916.

H Pownall Lieut R.A.

for ·············· Col. R.F.A
Comd'g 113th Brigade R.F.A.

1.10.16

To,
Headquarters,
   25th Division "A"

       Forwarded.
       E Cloete   Colonel, R.A.
6.10.16.   C.R.A. 25th Division.

Army Form C. 2118.

WAR DIARY
or
INTELLIGENCE SUMMARY.

(Erase heading not required.)

173 Brigade R.F.A. Vol 11

September

Place	Date	Hour	Summary of Events and Information	Remarks and references to Appendices
ST. LEGER	1st			
	4th		Brigade fired 180 rounds	
			Brigade fired about 1500 rounds on BOIS CARRÉ. Programme of Firing for to-day attered.	
	5th		Fired about 650 rounds according to Programme - New programmes of fire are going to be issued every day until further orders.	
	6th		Fired 430 rounds.	
	7th		"A" Battery are firing all to night along the edge of la BOIS DU CANAL to prevent enemy patrols coming out. "C" Battery are taking one gun forward to a position near FLANDRE by night. This position is within 1500 yds x of the German front line and the gun will be used for the "tirs des destruction". (See the Firing Programme.)	
	12th		Nothing unusual has occurred since the 7th - firing every day according to programme.	
		2.30 p.m.	About 12 5.9" Shells fell near to "C" Battery's position, two	

Army Form C. 2118.

113th Brigade RFA

WAR DIARY
or
INTELLIGENCE SUMMARY.
(Erase heading not required.)

Sept.

Place	Date	Hour	Summary of Events and Information	Remarks and references to Appendices
ST. LEGER	12th		of them falling very near the Officer's Mess. No casualties or damage to material.	
	16th		An A.S.C. Officer from G.H.Q. arrived in a car about mid-day. He has come down here for a few days to look into the question of Supplies. In the afternoon 2. Lieut STOBART of A.13 was wounded while reconnoitering a machine gun emplacement. He was taken to the American Hospital at ANNEL.	
	19th		Nothing to report since the 12th except the usual daily firing. 2. Lieut. STOBART received the Croix de Guerre from Général Bujolle, G.O.C. 81st Division Territoriale for successfully reconnoitering a machine gun emplacement.	
	21st		Small wood E. Boegneteau 31 - Shelled with 30 minenwerfer bombs.	
	24th		The Battery Positions here inspected this morning by General Humbert Commanding Third French Army. Colonel Maliver, Artillery Adviser to the 13th Army Corps was also	4

Army Form C. 2118.

1/3 Adv R.F.A
Sept 1916

WAR DIARY
or
INTELLIGENCE SUMMARY.
(Erase heading not required.)

Instructions regarding War Diaries and Intelligence Summaries are contained in F. S. Regs., Part II. and the Staff Manual respectively. Title pages will be prepared in manuscript.

Place	Date	Hour	Summary of Events and Information	Remarks and references to Appendices
ST LEGER	24th		Present - also Général Major C.R.A. Third French Army - Général Raythe G.O.C. 81e Division Territoriale and Lieut-Colonel d'Alayer C.R.A. 81e Divisional Artillery. We were informed - verbally - that it was probable that we should move in a few days.	
	25th		Batteries were inspected by Général Abry, Commanding 13e Corps d'Armée.	
	27th		Between 9.40 AM and 10 AM about 6 5.9 inch H.E. shells fell in and near Bois St Marc. 'B' and 'C' Batteries retaliated. At 5.30 PM an enemy aeroplane dropped several bombs on BAILLY - No damage -	
	28th		Enemy aeroplane dropped about 6 bombs near to BALCON O.P.	
	30th		Lieut Harris "A" Battery carried out a reconnaissance of the enemy position at Pont de la Rouille, examining in between the Wires on 15th inst.	

Saunders Col al
Cmdg 113 R.F.A

13ᵉ CORPS D'ARMÉE

ARTILLERIE
53ᵉ Régiment

Secteur Postal 98

Objet :
tir n° S/40

Aux Armées, le 3 Septembre 1916.

Le Lieutenant-Colonel d'Alayer de Costemore,
Commandant p. i. le 53ᵉ Régiment d'Artillerie,
à Monsieur le Major Commandant provisoirement
la 113ᵉ Brigade R.F.A.

Le Général Commandant le 13ᵉ C.A. fait connaître que le programme de tir sur le bois des Rigoles, présenté par la 81ᵉ Division, est approuvé sous réserve des modifications suivantes :

1°/ Etant donné la grande étendue du terrain à battre, la consommation en obus sera portée à :

    500 pour la batterie A.
    400   — d° ...... B
    400   — d° C

2°/ Les tirs à obus explosifs seront précédés de rafales d'obus fusants pour surprendre les ennemis aux abris. Allocation pour ce tir de surprise : 200 coups à balles.

3°/ Des mesures spéciales de sécurité devront être prises pendant les tirs de la batterie A. sur la mitrailleuse 5906, par suite de la proximité de nos lignes.

En conséquence la consommation de munitions prévue par le programme de tir n° S/40 sera augmentée et portée aux allocations fixées ci-dessus ; les rafales d'obus fusants précéderont chacune des phases du tir d'efficacité.

En outre je demande au Général Cdt la 162ᵉ Brigade de prescrire pendant l'exécution du tir l'évacuation de notre tranchée de 1ʳᵉ ligne dans le voisinage de l'Oise.

d'Alayer

13e CORPS D'ARMÉE

ARTILLERIE
53e Régiment

SECTEUR POSTAL 98

Objet :

tir n° 5/4.

Aux Armées, le 3 Août 1916 ~~1916~~. Sept

Le Lieutenant-Colonel d'Alayer de Costemore, Commandant p.'A.S.O. ~~le 53e Régiment d'Artillerie~~ à

Monsieur le Lt-Colonel Commandant la II3e Brigade R.F.A.

J'ai l'honneur de vous adresser ci-joint le programme d'un tir à exécuter par la II3e Brigade R.F.A. sur le Bois des Rigoles.
 Le tir d'efficacité sera exécuté le 4 Septembre, en trois phases, aux heures suivantes :
 1ère phase à 16 h, **50**
 2e phase à 17 h, 15
 3e phase à 18 h, 00
 Dans chaque phase les batteries agiront simultanément et rapidement pour obtenir un effet de surprise.

d'Alayer

13ᵉ Corps d'Armée
Secteur Ouest
ARTILLERIE

S/49

Le 4 septembre 1916

PROGRAMME des TIRS
pour la journée du 5 septembre
-o-o-o-o-o-o-o-o-o-o-o-o-o-o-o-o-

En dehors des tirs qui pourront être demandés par l'Infanterie, les tirs indiqués ci-après seront exécutés pendant la journée du 5 Septembre.

Objectifs et nature du tir	Allocation
Tir d'empoisonnement sur le Pont de la ROUILLY et le bois du Canal	
Tir d'empoisonnement sur le bois des Rigoles.	360 coups
Tir de destruction sur mitrailleuse de BAILLY Nord.	
Tir de destruction sur tranchées du Camp QUIN.	

Le Lt-COLONEL d'ALAYER
Cdt l'A.S.O.

[signature]

à M. le Commandant de la 113ᵉ Bᵈᵉ RFA

81e Division

162° Brigade

N° 3129

P.C. le 5 septembre 1916.

Le Général FELINEAU
Commandant la 162° Brigade Territoriale

à Monsieur le Major Commandant provisoirement la 113° Brigade d'Artillerie anglaise

PROGRAMME DES TIRS DE L'ARTILLERIE ANGLAISE
POUR LA JOURNEE DU 5 SEPTEMBRE.

(Comme suite à la Note S/49 du 4 septembre 1916 du Lieutenant-Colonel Commandant l'A/S.O.)

-:-:-:-:-:-

TIRS DE DESTRUCTION.

Objectifs : Mitrailleuse de Bailly-Nord et tranchées du Camp QUIN.

Consommation globale approximative : 300 coups.

Heure du tir : 17 h.45.

TIRS D'EMPOISONNEMENT.

Objectifs : Pont de la ROUILLY et Bois du Canal Bois des Rigoles.

Consommation globale approximative : 100 coups.

Tirer surtout la nuit, et en particulier de 19 h.30 à 21 heures, et au lever du jour.

13° Corps d'Armée
Secteur Ouest
Artillerie

p.C. le 5 Septembre 1916

PROGRAMME

des tirs systématiques à exécuter les 6 et 7 Septembre

A.D./81

1°.- Le 6 Septembre:

- Tir des canons de tranchée sur les emplacements de minenwerfer
  0695 (100 bombes) G.R. de Puisaleine lisière S du bois triangulaire
  2580 (120 bombes) Bascule de Quennevières
  8396 (120 bombes) Lisière sud du Bois du Grand Quesnoy
- Tir d'accompagnement par le 75 pendant le tir du 58/T.
- Tir de A/90 sur les tranchées 9397, lisière sud du bois des Haies Ballin (travaux signalés par la 162ème brigade).

2°.- le 7 septembre:

- Tir de destruction sur le Petit Curieux et le Grand Curieux (300 bombes)
- Tir sur minenwerfer 9196 (100 bombes) N-E de Tracy le Val.
- Tir d'accompagnement par le 75 pendant le tir du 58/T.

BATTERIES DE LA 113° B^{de} R.F.A.-

1°.- Le 6 Septembre: (environ 350 coups)

- Tirs de surprise sur les carrefours 6709, Bailly Nord; 7707 Bois de la Carbonnerie.
- Tirs de destruction sur les tranchées de 2ème ligne du Bois de la Carbonnerie.
- Tirs sur les tranchées au N. du Pont de la Rouilly.

2°.- Le 7 Septembre:

- Tir de destruction sur la tranchée de 2° ligne et les abris de la tranchée du Camp QUIN, notamment autour des points 6606 et 6704.
- Tir d'empoisonnement sur le Bois des Rigoles et sur la Quenotterie.

En cas de beau temps, réglage par avion et tir d'efficacité sur la batterie des Ecozieux. (rive dr. de l'Oise au N de Pimprez

Le Lt-Colonel d'ALAYER Cdt l'A.S.O.

Secteur Ouest. 　　　　　　　　　　　　　　Le 6 Septembre 1916

Artillerie.

PROGRAMME des tirs pour le 8 Septembre
-:-:-:-:-:-:-:-:-:-

113° Brigade R.F.A. - Tir de destruction sur boyaux:

　　6011 à 6114 (6114) - Boyau allant du Bois Carré à la tranchée des Étangs
　　6810 à 6913 - Boyau allant de Bailly à la Quenotterie
　　7109 à 7212 - Boyau allant de Bailly à la tranchée Auriol

　　　- Tir de surprise la nuit, sur les boyaux détruits.

　　　- Tir de surprise, le jour, sur
　　5614 (abris en lisière sud de la forêt d'Ourscamp).
　　7116 (abris près de la Quenotterie).

A.C.et A.T.　　　　Mitrailleuse et minen 2181
　　　　　　　　　(80 bombes; accompagnement par le 75
　　　　　　　　　Groupe Lachaud)

　　　　　　　　　Travaux et minen 9596
　　　　　　　　　(80 bombes; accompagnement par le 75
　　　　　　　　　Groupe Barberon)

　　　　　　　　　Travaux 9297 et minen 9196
　　　　　　　　　(80 bombes; accompagnement par le 75
　　　　　　　　　Groupe Tantin)

　　　　　　　　　　Le Lt-Colonel d'ALAYER Cdt l'A.S.O.

Approuvé.
Le Général Cdt la 11° Division,
signé: Bajolle

113° Brigade R.F.A.

Secteur Ouest   le 7 Septembre 1916

Artillerie

N°S/

PROGRAMME DES TIRS
pour le Neuf Septembre

1°.- 113ème Brigade R.F.A.

a - Tirs de destruction des ouvrages et tranchées:

1°.- Entre le Bois carré et Bailly (6110 à 6408)

2°.- Au Nord-Est de Bailly   (6708 à 6908)

Tirs de surprise la nuit, sur ces mêmes objectifs.

b - Eventuellement, tir de la pièce avancée (5092) sur les abris de mitrailleuses de la lisière S-E-du Bois-Carré.

ADDITIF AUX PROGRAMMES DES 7 & 8 SEPTEMBRE.-

Tirs de surprise pendant les nuits des 7 au 8 et 8 au 9 Septembre, sur la zône voisine du Pont de la Rouilly, et comprise entre le Canal et l'Oise.

A.D./81 et A.T.

---

a - Continuation des destructions:

1°.- Lisière S.bois des Haies Ballin (9297 et 9397)
(60 bombes; accompagnement par groupe Tantin).

2°.- Corne du Bois Triangulaire
(60 bombes; accompagnement par groupe Barberon).

b - Vérification des barrages du 58/T.
à une heure déterminée, tir simultané de 2 bombes par pièce.

Le Lt-Colonel d'ALAYER Cdt l'A.S.O

Destinataires:

Lt-Colonel A/D/81
Lt-Colonel 113°R.F.A.
Capitaine Cdt A.T.

Secteur Ouest

Artillerie

N° S/53

le 7 Septembre 1916

NOTE de SERVICE

Par ordre du Général Commandant la 81ème D.T.

La 113ème Brigade R.F.A. exécutera pendant les nuits des 7 au 8, et 8 au 9 septembre, sur la zône voisine du Pont de la Rouilly, comprise entre le Canal et la Boucle de l'Oise, des tirs de surprise par rafales, à intervalles irréguliers, pour interdire la circulation des patrouilles ennemies dans cette région.

OBJECTIFS PRINCIPAUX.-

    Pont de la Rouilly

    Bois du Canal

    Zône entre le Bois du Canal & l'Oise

Le Lt-Colonel d'ALAYER, Cdt l'A.S.O.

Destinataires: M. le Général Cdt la 81ème D.T. (à titre de compte-rendu)
     M. le Général Cdt la 162ème Brigade
     M. le Commandant de la 113ème Brigade R.F.A.

Secteur Ouest　　　　　　　　　　　　　　Le 8 Septembre 1916

Artillerie

N°.....

PROGRAMME DES TIRS

pour la journée du 10 Septembre

1°.- II3ème Brigade R.F.A.

a - Tir de destruction d'ouvrages de la 2ème ligne de tranchée de la Rouillette, (lisière Est du Bois de la Carbonnerie)

OBJECTIFS PRINCIPAUX.-

Tranchées et ouvrages 7502, 7303, 7307

Mitrailleuses 7502 et 7303.

b - Tir de surprise la nuit, sur ces mêmes objectifs et sur les points qui ont été antérieurement l'objet de tirs de destruction.

2°.- A.D./81 & A.T.

Tirs habituels suivant les circonstances et à la demande de l'Infanterie.

Le Lt-Colonel d'ALAYER Cdt l'A.S.O.

[signature]

Destinataires:

Lt-Colonel Cdt A.D./81
Lt-Colonel Cdt II3° Brigade R.F.A.
Capitaine Cdt A.T.

13° Corps d'Armée |PM| Le 9 Septembre 1916

Secteur Ouest

PROGRAMME DES TIRS pour le ~~10~~ Septembre (onze)

Artillerie

1°.- 113ème Brigade R.F.A.

a - Tir de destruction par la pièce avancée (5092), sur les ouvrages de la lisière S-E du Bois Carré :

    Mitrailleuse et abris 6108

    d°   d°   5906

b - Continuation des tirs de destruction sur les boyaux :

    du Bois Carré à la tranchée des Etangs (6011 à 6114) A

    de Bailly à la Quenotterie (6710 à 6913) B

c - Tir de surprise, la nuit, de quelques rafales sur les objectifs précités et sur ceux qui ont fait antérieurement l'objet de tirs de destruction.

2°.- A.D.81 et A.T.

a - Tir de destruction du minen, vers la lisière S-O du Bois des Haies Ballin, 9196.

    (A.T. 60 bombes, accompagnement par Gr. TANTIN)

b - Tir de destruction sur les ouvrages de la région de la Bascule (Ouvrages signalés par le prisonnier en 2380)

    (A.T. 100 bombes, accompagnement par GR. LAEHAUD)

c - Eventuellement, tir sur le minen au N de la Fosse Cadot en 0097, s'il continue à montrer de l'activité.

    (A.T. 80 bombes, accompagnement par gr. BARBERON).

Lt-Colonel Cdt A.D.81
Lt-Colonel Cdt 113° R.F.A.
Capitaine Cdt A.T.

                              Le Lt-Colonel d'ALAYER Cdt l'A.S.O.

Secteur Ouest　　　　　　　[4 PM]　　　　　Le 10 Septembre 1916

Artillerie　　　　PROGRAMME DES TIRS pour la journée du 12 Septembre

-:-:-:-:-:-:-:-:-:-:-:-:-:-:-:-:-

I°.- 113ème Brigade R.F.A.

-:-:-:-:-:-:-:-:-:-

a - Tir de destruction sur les ouvrages de la 2° ligne de tranchée à l'est de BAILLY.
    6606 à 6905

b - Tir de destruction des boyaux aboutissant à cette ligne de tranchée.
    6905 à 6908
    6606 à 6708

c - Tirs de surprise sur ces objectifs et sur ceux antérieurement battus.

-:-:-:-:-:-:-:-:-:-:-:-:-:-:-

2°.- A.D./81 et A.T.

a - Continuation des destructions d'ouvrages et de minen à la lisière S.O. du Bois des Haies Ballin:
    ouvrages 9297 et 9397
    minen............ 9197
    (80 bombes;accompagnement par le Groupe TANTIN.)

b - Pour le S/Secteur de COSNE, un programme sera transmis ultérieurement. Des objectifs intéressants ont été signalés par le Colonel Commandant la 186°Brigade, au Lt-Colonel Cdt l'A.D.81 et feront l'objet des prochains tirs.

Le Lt-Colonel d'ALAYER Cdt l'A.S.O.

Destinataires: M. le Lt-Colonel Cdt l'A.D.81
    M. le Lt-Colonel Cdt la 113°R.F.A.
    M. le Capitaine Cdt l'A.T.

Secteur Ouest   Le II Septembre 1916

Artillerie

ADDITIF au programme des TIRS pour la journée
du I2 Septembre I9I6.

A.D./8I et A.T.

Sous-Secteur de Cosnes.-

b - Tir de destruction sur les abris et ouvrages signalés
    par le prisonnier, en 22.80. (Région de la Bascule)
    (80 bombes, accompagnement par groupe LACHAUD).

c - Tir sur minenwerfer I990, au Nord de la Maison Rouge.
    (80 bombes, accompagnement par groupe LACHAUD.)

Le Lt-Colonel d'ALAYER Cdt l'A.S.O.

Destinataires: M. le Lt-Colonel Cdt la II3°Brigade R.F.A.
               M. le Lt-Colonel Cdt l'A.D.8I
               M. le Capitaine Cdt l'A.T.

In addition to shooting programme of the 12th September:
b - Destruction shooting on dugouts and works signaled by prisoner at 22.80
    (Neighbourhood of "La Bascule") 80 bombs, with group Lachaud

c - Shooting on trench mortars 1990, north of "Maison Rouge"
    (80 bombs, accompanied by group Lachaud)

Secteur Ouest   le 11 Septembre 1916

Artillerie

PROGRAMME DES TIRS pour la journée du 13 septembre

1°.- 113ème Brigade R.F.A.

a - Tir sur tranchées au N.du Pont de la Rouilly,et mitrailleuse signalée par l'Infanterie près du pont.

b - Tir de destruction sur les abris de la partie N.du Bois Carré 6010 et 6011.

c - Tir de surprise,la nuit,de quelques rafales,sur les objectifs précités.

Tir d'empoisonnement la nuit,par rafales de fusants pour surprendre le personnel ennemi circulant entre la Quénotterie et la sortie N.de Bailly.

2°.- A.D.81 et A.T.

a - Continuation des destructions d'ouvrages et de mines,à la lisière S-O-du Bois des Haies Ballin.
  ouvrages 9297 et 9397
  mines   9196
  (80 bombes;accompagnement par le groupe TANTIN)

b - Tir de destruction sur abri de mitrailleuse au S-de la Bascule en 25.79 (renseignements de prisonnier)
  (80 bombes;accompagnement par le groupe LACHAUD).
  50 coups de 120 court, batterie 497

c - Eventuellement,tir sur mines 1990,s'il continue à montrer de l'activité.
  (70 bombes;accompagnement par le Groupe LACHAUD).

Le Lt-Colonel d'ALAYER Cdt l'A.S.O.

Destinataires:M.le Lt-Colonel Cdt la 113°Brigade R.F.A.
              M.le Lt-Colonel Cdt l'A.D./81
              M.le Capitaine Cdt l'A.T.

13e CORPS D'ARMÉE

ARTILLERIE
53e Régiment

SECTEUR POSTAL 98

Objet :

n° 5/62

Aux Armées, le 12 Septembre 1916.

Le Lieutenant-Colonel d'Alayer de Costemore, Commandant p.i. A.S.O. ~~le 53e Régiment d'Artillerie~~, à Monsieur le Major commandant provisoirement la 113e Brigade R.F.A.

Par ordre du Général commandant la 71e Division, la 113e Brigade exécutera pendant les nuits des 12 au 13 et 13 au 14 Septembre, sur la zone au Sud du Pont de la Rouilly, comprise entre le canal et l'Oise, des tirs de surprise par rafales à intervalles irréguliers pour interdire la circulation des patrouilles ennemies dans cette région. (environ 100 coups par nuit.)

d'Alayer

Secteur ouest   Le 12 Septembre 1916

Artillerie   PROGRAMME DES TIRS POUR LA JOURNEE DU 14 SEPTEMBRE

1253

2.30

                            1°.- 113ème Brigade R.F.A.

a - Continuation des destructions d'ouvrages de 2° ligne et de boyaux, en
    particulier:
        ouvrage de la tranchée du Camp Quin   (6705 et 6905)
        ouvrage de la tranchée du Tenon   (6308 et 6110)
        noeuds de boyaux   (6908 et 6011)

b - Tir de surprise, la nuit, sur les objectifs précités.

    ADDITIF aux programmes des 12 et 13 Septembre 1916.-

    Tir de surprise pendant les nuits des 12 au 13 & 13 au 14 Septembre
        sur la zône voisine du Pont de la Rouilly entre le Canal
        et l'Oise.

                            2°.- A.D.81 et A.T.

a - Tir de destruction de minens de la lisière Sud du Bois du Grand
        Quesnoy.
        (70 bombes sur minen qui se révèlerait, accompagnement
        par le groupe TANTIN)

b - Tir de destruction sur les mitrailleuses de la région de Puisaleine
        2184
        2281
        (120 bombes; accompagnement par le groupe LACHAUD)

c - Eventuellement, tir de destruction sur les M.W. au Nord de la Fosse
        Cadot, en 0097 et 0197, s'ils montrent de l'activité.
        (70 bombes par minen; accompagnement par groupe BARBERON)

                                    Le Lt-Colonel d'ALAYER Cdt l'A.S.O.

Destinataires: M. le Lt-Colonel Cdt la 113° Brigade R.F.A.
               M. le Lt-Colonel Cdt l'A.D.81
               M. le Capitaine Cdt l'A.T.

Secteur Ouest   Le 13 Septembre 1916

Artillerie   PROGRAMME DES TIRS POUR LA JOURNEE DU 15 SEPTEMBRE

(4 pm)   1°.- II3°Brigade R.F.A.

S/SECTEUR de ST-LEGER.

 a - Continuation des destructions d'ouvrages de 2°ligne, en particulier;
   ouvrages de la tranchée du Camp Quin (6606-6705-6905) C
   ouvrage de la tranchée de Tenon   (6308-6110) B
   noeuds de boyaux   (6908-6011) B

 b - Tir de surprise, la nuit, sur les objectifs précités.

      2°.- A/D/81 et A.T.

 a - Surveillance des minens de la lisière Sud du Bois du Grand Quesnoy.
   (70 bombes sur minen qui se révèlerait, accompagnement par groupe TANTIN).

S/SECTEUR de COSNES.-

 b - Tir de destruction sur observatoire et lance-bombes de la région de la Bascule en 2381 (Renseignements de prisonnier
   (80 bombes, accompagnement par le groupe LACHAUD)

 c - Surveillance des minens du Coude de la chaussée Brunehaut.
   (tir de représailles par l'A.T. sur minen qui montrerait de l'activité; accompagnement par groupe BARBERON.)

      Le Lt-Colonel d'ALAYER Cdt l'A.S.O.

Destinataires: M. le Lt-Colonel Cdt l'A.D./81
      M. le Lt-Colonel Cdt la II3°Brigade R.F.A.
      M. le Capitaine Cdt l'A.T.

Secteur Ouest   Le 14 Septembre 1916

Artillerie   PROGRAMME DES TIRS pour la journée du 16 Septembre
                     ───

                            1°= 113ème Brigade R.F.A.
                            ─────────────────────────

S/Secteur de St-LEGER.-

   a - Continuation des destructions prévues par les program-
       mes des 14 et 15 Septembre.

   b - Tir de surprise sur noeuds de boyaux au N.E. de Bailly
       6913-7212-7109-5911

   c - Tir de surprise sur carrefours du Bois de la Carbonnerie
       7604-7706-7910.

                            A/D/81   et   A.T.
                            ──────────────────

   a - Surveillance des minens de la lisière S/du Bois du Grand
       Quesnoy.
       (70 bombes sur minen qui se révèlerait, accompagnement par groupe TANTIN).

S/Secteur de COSNES.-

   b - Tirs de destruction sur ouvrages et minens du Bois Trian-
       gulaire à lisière S.du Bois Triangulaire en
       0695.
       (80 bombes, accompagnement par Gr.BARBERON)

   c - Surveillance des minens au sud du Bois Barbu en 1890.
       (tir de représailles de l'A.T.et de l'A.C.
       (groupe LACHAUD) sur minen qui montrerait
       de l'activité.

   d - Eventuellement tir sur minen au N-de la Fosse Cadot en
       0097
       (70 bombes) accompagnement par gr.BARBERON)

   N O T A . - Le concours du 95 sera demandé pour les actions
               sur M.W., le C.A.ayant fait connaitre que ce
               calibre disposait d'allocations suffisantes.

Destinataires: Le Lt-Colonel d'ALAYER Cdt l'A.S.O.
M.le Lt-Colonel Cdt la 113°R.F.A.
M.le Lt-Colonel Cdt l'A.D./81
M.le Capitaine Cdt l'A.T.du S.O.

Secteur Ouest   10 am   Le 15 Septembre 1916

Artillerie

PROGRAMME DES TIRS pour la Journée du 17 Septembre

1°.- 115ème BRIGADE R.F.A.

S/SECTEUR de St-LEGER.-

 a - Continuation des destructions d'ouvrages de 2°ligne
   des tranchées de Tenon et du Camp Quin.

 b - Tir sur boyaux:
   1°.- Bois carré à Tranchée des Etangs
    (6011 à 6714)
   2°.- Bailly à Casnotterie
    (6700 à 6973)
   3°.- Bailly à Tranchée Amiot
    (7109 à 7212)

 c - Tirs de surprise, la nuit, sur les objectifs précités.

2°.- A/D/81 et A/T/

 a - Surveillance des minens de la lisière S. du Bois du
   Grand Quesnoy.
   (VO bombes sur minen qui se révèlerait, ac-
   compagnement par le groupe TANTIN.)

S/SECTEUR DE COSNE.-

 b - Surveillance des minens de la région du Bois Barbu,
   en particulier : 1691,1693,1890,1891.
   (tirds destruction par l'A.T.et l'A.C.sur minen qui montrerait de l'activité.Coopération
   du 120 C.et du 95(Batterie 50 P) pour renforcer l'action de l'A.T.et de l'A.C.)

       Le Lt-Colonel d'ALAYER Cdt l'A.S.O.

Destinataires: M.le Lt-Colonel Cdt la 115 Brigade R.F.A.
    M.le Lt-Colonel Cdt l'A.D.81
    M.le Capitaine Cdt l'A.T.de l'A.S.O.

Secteur Ouest   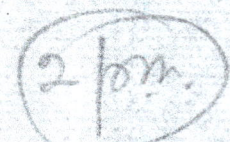   Le 16 Septembre 1916

Artillerie

PROGRAMME des TIRS pour la journée du 18 Septembre

I°.- II3ème brigade R.F.A.

S/SECTEUR de St-LEGER.-

B   a - Tir de destruction sur travaux nouveaux à la lisière S.E. du Bois Carré, vers le point 6007.

A   b - Tir sur mitrailleuse du Pont de la Rouilly et sur tranchées au N.du Pont.

     c - Continuation des tirs sur boyaux(tirs prévus par le paragraphe b du programme de la journée du 17)

     d - Tirs de surprise, la nuit, sur les objectifs précités.

A/D/81 et A.T.

----

     a - Surveillance des minens de la lisière S.du Bois du Grand Quesnoy.
         (70 bombes sur minen qui se révèlerait, accompagnement par le groupe TANTIN).

S/SECTEUR DE COSNE.-

     b - Surveillance des minens de la région du Bois Barbu, en particulier; 1691, 1693, 1890, 1891.
         (tir de destruction par l'A.C.et l'A.T. sur minen qui montrerait de l'activité.Coopération du 120 C. et du 95(Bie 50 P.)pour renforcer l'action de l'A.T. et de l'A.C.)

     c - Tir de destruction sur mitrailleuse au N.du Champignon, vers 1692.
         (70 bombes, accompagnement par le groupe BARBERON)

Le Lt-Colonel d'ALAYER Cdt l'A.S.O.

Destinataires: M.le Lt-Colonel Cdt la II3°Brigade R.F.A.
                M.le Lt-Colonel Cdt l'A.D./81
                M.le Capitaine Cdt l'A.T.de l'A.S.O.

Secteur Ouest 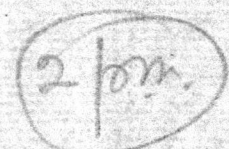 Le 16 Septembre 1916

Artillerie

PROGRAMME des TIRS pour la journée du 18 Septembre

1°.- 113ème brigade R.F.A.

S/SECTEUR de St-LEGER.-

B   a - Tir de destruction sur travaux nouveaux à la lisière S.E. du Bois Carré, vers le point 6007.

A   b - Tir sur mitrailleuse du Pont de la Rouilly et sur tranchées au N. du Pont.

c - Continuation des tirs sur boyaux (tirs prévus par le paragraphe b du programme de la journée du 17)

d - Tirs de surprise, la nuit, sur les objectifs précités.

A/D/81 et A.T.

---

a - Surveillance des minens de la lisière S. du Bois du Grand Quesnoy.
(70 bombes sur minen qui se révèlerait, accompagnement par le groupe TANTIN).

S/SECTEUR DE COSNE.-

b - Surveillance des minens de la région du Bois Barbu, en particulier; 1691, 1693, 1890, 1891.
(tir de destruction par l'A.C. et l'A.T. sur minen qui montrerait de l'activité. Coopération du 120 C et du 95 (Bie 50 P.) pour renforcer l'action de l'A. et de l'A.C.)

c - Tir de destruction sur mitrailleuse au N. du Champignon, 1692.
(70 bombes, accompagnement par le groupe BARBERON)

Le Lt-Colonel d'ALAYER Cdt l'A.S.O.

Destinataires: M. le Lt-Colonel Cdt la 113°Brigade R.F.A.
M. le Lt-Colonel Cdt l'A.D./81
M. le Capitaine Cdt l'A.T. de l'A.S.O.

Secteur Ouest   (3 p/m)   Le 16 Septembre 1916

Artillerie
───────────
PROGRAMME DES TIRS pour la journée du 20 SEPTEMBRE.

1°.- II5ème Brigade R.F.A.

S/Secteur St-LEGER.-

    a - continuation des tirs de destruction sur ouvrages de 2°
        ligne et sur boyaux(destructions prévues par les
        programmes antérieurs.

    b - Tirs de surprise sur convois,au N.de Pimprez.
        (roulement entendus tous les soirs vers 20 h.30'

    c - Tirs de surprise sur la lisière O.du Bois Carré,d'où l'
        ennemi lance des grenades sur le C.R.de l'Oise.
        Eventuellement,tirs de riposte si l'infanterie
        signale le lancement de grenades.

    d - Tirs de surprise,la nuit sur les objectifs qui auront fait
        l'objet de tirs de destruction.

2°.- A.D.81 et A.T.

    a - Surveillance des mines de la lisière Sud du Bois du
        Grand Quesnoy.
        (70 bombes sur mines qui se révèlerait,accompagnement
        par le groupe TANTIN.)

S/Secteur de COSNES.-

    b - Tir de destruction sur mines actifs de Poissaleine
        2165-2294
        ;(80 bombes,accompagnement par le groupe LACHAUD)

    c - Surveillance des mines de la région de la Chaussée
        Brunehaut 1291 et 1394
        (70 bombes sur mines qui montrerait de l'activité
        accompagnement par groupe BARBERON

        Le Lt-Colonel d'ALAYER Cdt l'A.S.O.

Destinataires:M. le Lt-Colonel Cdt l'A..../81
        M. le Lt-Colonel Cdt la II5°Brigade R.F.A.
        M. le Capitaine Cdt l'A.T.

Secteur Ouest   Le 19 Septembre 1916

Artillerie

PROGRAMME des TIRS pour la JOURNEE DU 21 SEPTEMBRE

1°.- 113° Brigade R.F.A.

S/Secteur de St-LEGER.-

   a - Continuation des destructions d'ouvrages de 2° ligne et
           des tirs sur boyaux (voir programmes antérieurs)

   b - Tirs de surprise le soir sur les convois à la sortie N.
           de Ecurex.

   c - Surveillance de la lisière O. du Bois Carré.

   d - Tirs de surprise, la nuit, sur les objectifs qui ont fait
           l'objet de tirs de destruction.

2°.- A.D.61 et A.T.

   a - Surveillance des mineurs de la lisière S. du Bois du Grand
           Quesnoy.
           (70 bombes sur mines qui se révèlerait, accom-
           pagnement par le groupe TANRIN.)

S/Secteur de COSNES.-

   b - Surveillance des mineurs de Puisaleine 2783-2185-2234.
           (tir de destruction par l'A.T. sur mines qui
           montrerait de l'activité, accompagnement par le
           Groupe LACHAUD.

   Eventuellement tir de représailles par l'A.T. et l'A.C.
           sur mines du Bois Baron.

                                   Le Lt-Colonel d'ALAYER Cdt l'A.S.O.

                                   signé: d'Alayer

Secteur Ouest.
Artillerie.

Le 20 Septembre 1916

PROGRAMME des TIRS pour la journée du 22 Septembre

(2)

I°. - 113° BRIGADE R.F.A.

S/Secteur de St-Léger.

 a - Continuation des destructions d'ouvrages de 2° ligne, en particulier de l'ouvrage 6110 (N.E. du Bois Carré) où des travaux sont signalés.

 b - Tirs de surprise sur les boyaux aboutissant au N. de BAILLY et au N. du Bois Carré.

 c - Surveillance de la lisière O. du Bois Carré.

 d - Tirs de surprise, la nuit, sur les convois à la sortie N. de PIMPREZ et sur les objectifs qui ont fait l'objet de tirs de destructions.

2°. - A.D.81 et A.T.

 a - Surveillance des minens de la lisière S. du Bois du Grand Carsney.
  (tir de destruction par l'A.T. sur minen qui se révèlerait; accompagnement par le Groupe TANTIN)

S/Secteur de Cenne.

 b - Surveillance générale des minens du S/Secteur.
  (Représailles par l'A.T. et l'A.C. sur minen qui montrerait de l'activité)

Le Lt-Colonel d'ALAYER Cdt. l'A.S.O.

DESTINATAIRES:
M. le Lt-Colonel Cdt. l'A.D.81.
 le Lt-Colonel Cdt. la 113°Bde R.F.A.
 le Capitaine Cdt. l'A.T. du Secteur.

Secteur ouest   Le 21 Septembre 1916

Artillerie   PROGRAMME de tir pour le 23 Septembre 1916

1°.- 113ème Brigade R.F.A.

S/Secteur St-LEGER.-

    a - Surveillance de la lisière S.de la forêt d'Ourscamp, vers le point 54I4,où est signalé un minen tirant sur le petit poste du boqueteau 3I.

    b - Tirs de surprise le soir,sur convois à la sortie Nord de Pimprez.

    c - Tirs de surprise,la nuit,sur les objectifs qui ont fait antérieurement l'objet de tirs de destruction.

2°.- A.D.8I et A.T.

    a - Surveillance des minens de la lisière Sud du Bois du Grand Quesnoy.

        Représailles par l'A.T.sur minen qui se révèlerait accompagnement par groupe TANTIN.

    b - Eventuellement,tir de surprise sur vagonnets au N.du Bois du Grand Quesnoy vers(85.00 - 84.02);si des bruits de roulement sont entendus dans cette région.

S/Secteur de COSNES.-

    c - Surveillance générale des minens du S/Secteur. (Représailles par l'A.T.et l'A.C.sur minen qui montrerait de l'activité.

                                Le Lt-Colonel d'ALAYER Cdt l'A.S.O.

Destinataires:M.le Lt-Colonel Cdt la 113°Brigade R.F.A.
               M.le Lt-Colonel Cdt l'A.D./8I
               M.le Capitaine Cdt l'A.T.de l'A.S.O.

Le 23 septembre 1918

Secteur Ouest

Artillerie   PROGRAMME DES TIRS pour la journée du 24 SEPTEMBRE
_____   _____

                              I° - IIIème Brigade R.F.A.

S/Secteur de St-LEGER.-

   a - Surveillance de la lisière Sud de la Forêt d'Ourcamp,mines
       vers 5414.

   b - Tirs de surprise, la nuit, sur convois au Nord de Flmpres et
       sur les objectifs qui ont fait antérieurement l'
       objet de tirs de destruction.

                              _____

                              A.D./6X et A.T.
                              _____

   a - Surveillance des mines à la lisière Sud du Bois du Grand
       Quesnoy et de la lisière S.O.du Bois des Haies
       Ballin.
       (Représailles par l'A.T.sur mines qui se révéle-
       rait,accompagnement par le groupe TANTIN).

   b - Tir de destruction sur mitrailleuse de la tranchée des
       Ecoutures 7299 par la section de 80 de M.
       (Section à l'Ouest de Nervaise).

S/Secteur de GOSIHES.-

   c - Surveillance générale des mines du S/Secteur.
       (Représailles par l'A.T.et l'A.C.sur mines qui
       montrerait de l'activité.

                                    Le Lt-Colonel d'ALAYER Cdt l'A.S.O.

                                         [signature]

Destinataires: M.le Lt-Colonel Cdt la IIIème Brigade R.F.A
              M.le Lt-Colonel Cdt l'A.D./6X
              M.le Capitaine Cdt l'A.T. de l'A.S.O.

Secteur Ouest   Le 27 Septembre 1916

Artillerie

PROGRAMME DES TIRS POUR LA JOURNEE DU 28 SEPTEMBRE
_____

I°. - III° Brigade R.F.A.
_____

S/Secteur St-LEGER.-

   Surveillance du front et continuation des tirs de surprise, la nuit, sur tranchées de 3°ligne, boyaux et
front de la Rouilly.

2°. - A/D/81 et A.T.
_____

a - Surveillance des mineurs du Bois du Grand Quesnoy
    (représailles par l'A.T., accompagnement par
    le groupe TANTIN).

S/Secteur de COSNES.-

b - Tir de l'A.T. sur ouvrages nouveaux du Saillant du
    Champignon (1691 - 1790).
    (80 bombes, accompagnement groupe LACHAUD)

c - Surveillance des mineurs du front du S/Secteur.
    (représailles par A.T. et A.C.)

                    Le Lt-Colonel d'ALANER Cdt l'A.S.O.

                         [signature]

Destinataires: M. le Lt-Colonel Cdt la III° Brigade R.F.A.
               M. le Lt-Colonel Cdt l'A.D./81
               M. le Capitaine Cdt l'A.T. de l'A.S.O.

Secteur Ouest   Le 24 Septembre 1916

Artillerie
                                                                    bre
                PROGRAMME DES TIRS POUR LES JOURNEES DES 25 et 26 Sept =

                        I°.- II3° Brigade R.F.A.

S/Secteur de St-LEGER.-

        a.- Surveillance du front, tirs de surprise, et tirs à la
            demande de l'Infanterie.

                        2°.- A/D/8I   et A.T.

        a.- Surveillance des mines du Bois du Grand Quesnoy.
                (représailles par l'A.T. accompagnement groupe
                TANPIN).

S/Secteur de COSNES.-

        b.- Surveillance des mines du front du S/Secteur.
                (représailles par A.T. et A.C.)

                        p. Le Lt-Colonel d'ALAYER Cdt l'A.S.O.

                        p.o Le Capitaine adjt.

IIIe Armée
Etat Major
3e Bureau

No. 793/3

Q.G.A. le 26 Septembre 1916.

Ordre Général No. 257 OP.

Au moment où les 64e et 113e Brigades de la Royal-Field-Artillery sont appelées à de nouvelles et glorieuses destinées, le Général Commandant la IIIe Armée se fait un devoir de remercier M.M. les Lieutenants-Colonels LAMBARDE et BARTON, ainsi que les Officiers et les canonniers sous leurs ordres, du précieux concours qu'ils ont prêté pendant quatre mois à leurs camarades Français.

Ceux-ci conserveront un profond souvenir de la belle confraternité d'armes qui n'a cessé de se manifester en toutes circonstances entre les troupes alliées luttant pour la même noble cause.

Le Général voit partir avec regret cette Artillerie magnifique dont la tenue a fait l'admiration de tous, qui a su en peu de temps, par sa vigilance, sa solide instruction et l'efficacité de ses tirs, mériter la confiance de l'Infanterie qu'elle avait mission d'appuyer.

Ses vœux ne cesseront de l'accompagner sur le champ de bataille plus actif où elle pourra sous l'aile de la victoire, donner toute sa mesure, déployer toute sa virtuosité, et contribuer efficacement au prochain triomphe des armes alliées.

Signé. HUMBERT

25th. DIVISIONAL ARTILLERY

113th. BRIGADE R. F. A.

25th. DIVISIONAL ARTILLERY

O C T O B E R   1 9 1 6.

WAR DIARY or INTELLIGENCE SUMMARY

Army Form C. 2118.

VOL 12

113 Brigade R.F.A. attached 81st Div. XIII Corps III French Army.

OCTOBER

Place	Date 1916	Hour	Summary of Events and Information	Remarks and references to Appendices
ST. LEGER aux Bois	Oct 2	About 12.45 pm	About 6 15cm H.E. fell in front of 'C' Battery's position. Same number again in same place at 7.45 pm.	
	3	2.30 pm	6 15cm H.E. fell in front of Battery's positions.	
Crisse Compiegne	4	11.40 am	6 15cm H.E. fell in front of Battery's positions	
	5	About 1 pm	12 15cm H.E. fell in the Battery positions. One man in B. 113 wounded. One of the dug-outs at the Central Telephone Exchange was blown in.	
	6		Received notification that Brigade will entrain during the night of October 9/10.	
	7		One Section of 'A' and one Section of 'C' Battery relieved to night	
	8		'A' Battery handed over Gun position to a French Colonial Battery and 'C' Battery handed over to a Battery of the 43rd Regiment d'Artillerie Française. 'B' Battery's position not being taken over.	
	9		All Batteries with own guns from action at 4 am. to Wagon Lines at LE PLESSIS BRION. Lieut. Col. F.F. LAMBARDE D.S.O. received the Croix de Guerre from G.O.C. 81st Division.	

Army Form C. 2118.

WAR DIARY
or
INTELLIGENCE SUMMARY
(Erase heading not required.)

113 Bde RFA

Place	Date	Hour	Summary of Events and Information	Remarks and references to Appendices
	9		H.Q. and 'A' Battery entrained at COMPIEGNE at 12 midnight Oct. 9/10.	
	10		H.Q. and 'A' left COMPIEGNE at 4.30 am 'B' and 'E' Batteries left at 8.30 am and 12.30 noon respectively - Brigade arrived at DOULLENS from 4 pm onwards - Billeted for the night at AUTHIEULE (just S.E. of DOULLENS)	
	11		Marched to wagon lines at USNA HILL near ALBERT.	
	12		Reconnoitered positions for Batteries near LE MOUQUET FARM.	
		4.20 pm	Received orders to go into action here during the night and to be ready for an operation.	
		4.45 pm	Orders cancelled and ordered to be in readiness to go into action N. of the R. ANCRE.	
	13		Ordered to join the 39th Div. Arty. Received instructions to take over positions of 83rd Bde. R.F.A. S. of THIEPVAL, which were reconnoitred.	

Army Form C. 2118.

WAR DIARY
or
INTELLIGENCE SUMMARY
(Erase heading not required.)

113½ B ott R.F.A.

Place	Date	Hour	Summary of Events and Information	Remarks and references to Appendices
	14		Orders cancelled. Received instructions to take over positions of 82nd Bde. R.F.A. in same area as HQ 83rd Bde. R.F.A. and to exchange guns. Everything to be completed by 10 pm 16. night. At 9.55 pm after exchange had been completed orders were cancelled and we were instructed to withdraw to wagon lines next morning. Assisted in attack on SCHWABEN REDOUBT. Successful.	
	15		Withdrew to Wagon Lines.	
	16		Received Orders that Brigade was to be attacked to 18th Div: Reconnoitred positions at MESNIL. Orders cancelled.	
		2 pm	Received orders to reconnoitre positions about R 33 b - 34 a (Map 57 D SE 1/20000) Brigade to entrain from R 22 b 06 to R 23 a 36 by her. evening.	
		6 pm	Orders issued to Batteries to go into action this evening.	
	17		Brigade HQ. in Quarry about 400ˣ S. of MOUQUET FARM. Batteries carried out registration of wire. 2 Gunners in "A" Battery wounded -	

Place	Date	Hour	Summary of Events and Information	Remarks and references to Appendices
	18		Batteries fired about 3000 rounds on wire in front of REGINA TR. 4 Signallers (HQ.) - 1 orderly (attached HQ.) from B.113 - 1 man of A.113 wounded.	
	19		Batteries fired on wire by day and night to prevent enemy repairing it	
	20		Wire-cutting in front of REGINA TR. Operations against GRANDCOURT TRENCH (R.16 b) which were to have taken place to-day postponed for 24 hours. Batteries fired 10 rds. per hour throughout the day on wire - 50 rds. per Battery during the night. In the afternoon 'C' Battery were shelled by a 15cm Howr. No casualties or damage.	
	21		Operations against REGINA TR. Zero hour 12.6 noon. Completely successful - Wire was reported well cut. 2 casualties - B.113. Operation Orders attached. Batteries now fire 50 rds. every night according to programme issued from HQ. 25th Div. Arty.	

Vol XIV

Army Form C. 2118.

WAR DIARY
or
INTELLIGENCE SUMMARY

(Erase heading not required.)

112 A Bde RFA

Place	Date	Hour	Summary of Events and Information	Remarks and references to Appendices
	22		Batteries expended 2400 rds on wire. Entering in front of GRANDCOURT trench (R 16 b)	
	23		Daily bombardment 6 am to 6.15 am. Wire kept under fire throughout the day.	
	24		Batteries fired 10 rds per hour throughout the day on wire. Wagon line was shelled about 12 noon with 4.2 in. - about 6 shells altogether - no casualties or damage. One man C.113 wounded.	
	25		Wire kept under fire day and night. 1 casualty A.113	
	26		Brigade fired about 250 rounds. One man killed A. 113	
	27		'A' and 'B' Batteries shelled with 7.7 cm yesterday afternoon and this morning. Batteries kept wire under fire. 2 Lieut McNEIL A.113 wounded	

Army Form C. 2118.

WAR DIARY
or
INTELLIGENCE SUMMARY
(Erase heading not required.)

112/H/Bde RFA

Place	Date	Hour	Summary of Events and Information	Remarks and references to Appendices
	28		Intermittent shelling by the enemy. A.113 shelled all morning and afternoon by 7.7 cm. Several 15 cm. shells fell in and around the Battery also. One gun A.113 hit, damage to Trail and Dial Sight. 2 Lieut HARRIS. A.113. wounded, one man A.113 wounded. 2 Lieuts MAYNE and COUPLAND-SMITH joined Brigade from England and posted to A.113.	
	29		Were kept under fire throughout the day.	
	31		'B' Battery's O.P. in ZOLLERN TRENCH was shelled in the afternoon one man being killed and Lieut. MILLER. B.113. wounded. Battery positions were shelled during the afternoon up till 10.30 pm with 15 cm, 10.5 cm and 7.7 cm shells. 15 cm lean shells were also used from 7 pm to 10.30 pm.	

J. [signature]
au[?] [signature]
O.C. 113 Bty. R.F.A.

IIIᵉ Armée
13ᵉ Corps d'Armée
Artillerie
N° 6373

Q.G. le 8 octobre 1916

Le Colonel MALESSET
Commandant p.i. l'Artillerie du 13ᵉ Corps d'Armée
à Monsieur le Lieut. Colonel LAMBARDE
Commandant la 113ᵉ Brigade d'Artillerie
Britannique.
s/c. de Monsieur le Général Commandant
le 13ᵉ Corps d'Armée.

Au moment où la 113ᵉ Brigade d'Artillerie Britannique quitte le Secteur OUEST du 13ᵉ C.A. j'ai l'honneur de vous adresser tous mes remerciements pour les excellents services qu'elle a rendu au cours de son séjour dans la zone du 13ᵉ C.A.

Sous le Commandement d'Officiers d'Artillerie d'une grande compétence, d'un zèle et d'une activité inlassables la 113ᵉ Brigade R.F.A. a donné à tous ceux qui l'ont vue à l'œuvre l'impression d'une troupe ayant une tenue et une discipline parfaites.

Le bon fonctionnement de ses liaisons, la vigilance de ses observateurs, la précision de ses tirs et la promptitude avec laquelle ils ont été déclanchés ont donné à notre Infanterie une entière confiance dans le concours de leurs camarades de l'Armée Britannique.

Signé   MALESSET.

[OVER]

Vu et transmis.
Le Général Commandant le 13ᵉ C.A. s'associe pleinement au témoignage de satisfaction formulée par le Colonel Commandant l'Artillerie du Corps d'Armée et est très heureux de remercier personnellement le Lieut-Colonel LAMBARDE et sa Brigade d'Artillerie des excellents services qu'ils ont rendu sur le front du 13ᵉ Corps.

9.10.16

Signé
GEN. ALBY

Adieux du Colonel d'Alayer de Costemore
Commandant d'Artillerie S.O. - 81ᵉ D.T.
  à la 113ᵉ Brigade R.F.A.
   le 9 octobre 1916

It is to my lively regret that I part company, to-day from the 113ᵗʰ Brigade R.F.A., whom I had the honour to work with for three months and a half.

During that period, I have been glad to get acquainted with our comrades of the British Army: I appreciated very much their high military qualities, their courtesy, their eagerness in supporting our Infantry by the swiftness and the precision of their firing. I admired the fair appearance of your men, horses and guns.

You are now going to a more busy zone: you will be there at quarters of honour and we may be sure that you will do a good work.

We shall hear from here the boom of your far distant cannonade and think of the gallant fellows of the British Army who fight hand in hand with us for the triumph of our mutual cause.

   GOD GRANT YOU MAY LEAD TO VICTORY
Our fondest wishes are to be with you anywhere sounds the report of your guns.
   "Ubique quo fas et gloria ducunt"
as says the lofty motto of the Royal Field Artillery.

IIIᵉ Armée
13ᵉ Corps d'Armée
81ᵉ Division I.T.
   État-Major

P.G. le 9 octobre 1916

ORDRE GENERAL N° 132

Le Général Commandant la 81ᵉ Division Territoriale cite à l'ordre de la Division les militaires dont les noms Suivent :

Le Lieutenant-Colonel LAMBARDE Commandant la 113ᵉ Brigade d'Artillerie de l'Armée Anglaise :

"Détaché avec sa Brigade d'Artillerie dans un Secteur français, a rendu les plus grands Services, par le concours absolu, de tous les instants, qu'il a donné à notre Infanterie. A fait preuve en toute circonstance de la meilleure Camaraderie de Combat. Officier supérieur très distingué, d'une grande bravoure, très méritant."

Le Général Commandant
la 81ᵉ Division.

Signé. BAJOLLE.

SECRET   Copy No. 19

25th DIVISIONAL ARTILLERY OPERATION ORDER No. 72

Reference Trench Maps   17th October, 1916.
1/5,000.

---

1. The 74th and 75th Infantry Brigades, 25th Division, at Zero, on October 19th, will attack REGINA Trench between R.23.a.0.3. and R.21.a.7.5. - STUMP ROAD to R.21.a.6.7. - STUFF trench from R.21.a.6.7. to R.20.b.9.6.

2. 18th Division will attack REGINA trench Eastwards of R.23.a.0.3.
   39th Division will attack STUFF trench Westwards of R.20.b.9.6.

3. Zero hour will be notified later.

4. Brigade objectives will be as follows :-

   74th Inf. Bde- REGINA trench from R.23.a.0.3. to R.22.a.3.8.   (roadway inclusive)

   75th Inf. Bde- REGINA trench from R.22.a.3.8. (roadway exclusive) - STUMP road and STUFF trench to R.20.b.9.6. (inclusive)

5. The attack will start from the line HESSIAN trench - R.21.a.8.0. - c.5.8., 3.8.1.8.
   Advanced posts in front of this line and within 200 yards of the Divisional objective, will be withdrawn prior to the attack.

6. 75th Infantry Brigade will extend its right to R.22.c.3.7. Extension to be completed by 12 noon October 18th.

7. 25th Divisional Artillery will fire according to table which will be issued later.

8. ACKNOWLEDGE.

                                                    M. Enlle.
                                                    Major, R.A.
                                              Bde Major, 25th Divl. Artillery

Issued at 10 a.m.

     Copies to :-
              O.C. 110th Bde. R.F.A.
                   111th Bde.   "
                   112th Bde.   "
                   113th Bde.   "
                   25th D.A.C.

S E C R E T.   B.M.654.

O.C.110th Brigade.R.F.A.
O.C.111th   "   "
O.C.112th   "   "
O.C.113th   "   "
----

1. Reference 25th Div.Arty Operation Order 72.
   ZERO hour for the attack on REGINA trench is 12-6.p.m.
(twelve six p.m.) today, October 21st.
   This hour will only be communicated to those directly
concerned.
   No mention of the word Zero is to be made on the
telephone.
   The hour is to be communicated to those concerned as
late as possible.

2. Brigades detailed for wire cutting along REGINA trench
will continue to do so from 8-30 a.m. up to ZERO hour.

3. All known or suspected hostile Machine Gun
position will be bombarded by 4.5" Hows between 9.0.a.m. and
12 noon

4. ACKNOWLEDGE.

                                           Major. R.A.
21-10-1916.   Brigade Major, 25th Div. Arty.

Page 1.

25th DIVISIONAL ARTILLERY OPERATION ORDER No. 72.
TIME TABLE FOR 18 Pdr. GUNS.

UNIT.	TIME.	OBJECTIVE.	Rate of fire.
112th Bde.R.F.A. All guns.	Zero to 0.1½	R.22.a.8015-0025-R.21.b.7.2.	
	0.1½ to 0.3	R.22.c.8.3.-R.21.b.8545- 7045	
	0.3 to 0.6	R.22.c.8.7.- R.21.b.7055	
	0.6 onwards	Roll back at rate of 100 yds per minute to the line R.16.c.8.1. - R.21.b.7095	
111th Bde.R.F.A. 4 18 pdr.guns.	Zero to 0.1½	R.21.b.7.2. - 3015	Zero to 0.10 4 rounds per gun per minute.
	0.1½ to 0.3	R.21.b.7045 - 3.4.	0.10 to 0.25 2 rounds per gun per minute.
	0.3 to 0.6	R.21.b.7055 - 3.4.	0.25 to 0.40 1 round per gun per minute.
	0.6 onwards	Roll back at rate of 100 yds per minute to the line R.21.b.7095 - 3085.	
111th Bde.R.F.A. Less 4 guns.	Zero to 0.6	REGINA trench R.21.b.7555 - 3.4.	0.40 onwards, watch situation closely; fire to be opened immediately if required.
	0.6 onwards	Roll back at rate of 100 yds per minute to line R.15.d.7.0. - R.21.b.30.85	

25th DIVISIONAL ARTILLERY OPERATION ORDER No. 72.
TIME TABLE FOR 18 PR. GUNS.

Page 2.

UNIT.	TIME.	OBJECTIVE.	Rate of fire.
113th Bde. R.F.A. All guns.	Zero to 0.6	REGINA trench R.22.a.8.7.-1575	
	0.6 onwards	Roll back at rate of 100 yds per minute to R.16.c.8.1.-1515.	Zero to 0.10 4 rounds per gun per minute.
110th Bde. R.F.A. 8 guns.	Zero to 0.6	REGINA trench R.22.a.1575 - R.21.b.7555.	0.10 to 0.25 2 rounds per gun per minute. 16 - 31
	0.6 onwards	Roll back at rate of 100 yds per minute to line R.16.c.1515 - R.15.d.7.0.	0.25 to 0.40 1 round per gun per minute. 31 - 46
110th Bde. R.F.A. 4 guns.	Zero to 0.6	Search and sweep the area R.22.a.8.7. - R.16.c.8.1. - R.21.b.3085 - 5.4.	0.40 onwards, watch situation closely; fire to be opened immediately if required.
	0.6 onwards	R.16.c.8.1. - R.21.b.3085	

25th DIVISIONAL ARTILLERY OPERATION ORDER No. 72
TIME TABLE FOR 4.5" Hows.

UNIT.	TIME.	OBJECTIVE.	Rate of fire.
D/110	Zero to 0.1½	R.22.a.4.8. – R.16.c.4.1.	Zero to 0.10 2 rounds per How. per minute
	0.1½ to 0.3	R.16.c.4.0. – 5.6.	
	0.3 to 0.6	Roll back at rate of 50 yds per minute to R.16.c.5535-6.6.–4.8.	0.10 to 0.25 1 round per How. per minute.
	0.6 onwards	R.16.c.5535 – 6.6. – 4.8.	
D/111	Zero onwards	Dug outs R.15.d.2.9.–R.15.b.4.4.	0.25 to 0.40 1 round per How. per 2 minutes.
D/112	Zero onwards	New trench R.15.c.9.3. – 5340	0.40 onwards, watch situation closely; fire to be opened immediately if required.

S E C R E T.

ADDENDUM No.1. to 25th DIVISIONAL ARTY OPERATION ORDER No.72.

18th October, 1916.

---

1. From 0.15 onwards, Brigade Commanders of 110th, 111th, and 112th Brigades will arrange that one Battery responds to all N.F. targets within range.

2. ACKNOWLEDGE.

[signature]
Major, R.A.
Brigade Major, 25th Divl Arty.

Copies to all recipients of 25th D.A. Operation Order No.72.

S E C R E T

ADDENDUM No. 2 to 25th Div.Arty O.O.72

18th October 1916.

1. Troops on the extreme right and left of the Divisional front will carry red flags to indicate their positions to 53rd Inf. Bde, 18th Divn, on the right, and to 116th Inf.Bde, 39th Divn., on the left.

2. A contact aeroplane will fly over the area of attack from zero. Infantry will light flares and wave helmets and flags at zero plus thirty minutes, and again at zero plus one hour, and at any time when the aeroplane lights a white flare or sounds a Klaxon horn.

3. Patrols will be pushed forward to the limits allowed by the artillery protective barrage directly the objective has been gained, and posts will be established at all important tactical points.

4. ACKNOWLEDGE.

Major, R.A.
Bde Major, 25th Divl.Artillery

Copy to all recipients of 25th Div.Arty Op.Order No.72.

S E C R E T.

ADDENDUM No.3 to 25th DIV ARTY OPERATION ORDER No.72.

<u>19th October, 1916.</u>

1.   Reference paras 1 & 4 of 25th Div. Arty Operation Order No.72, the Eastern boundary of the objective of 74th Infantry Brigade, 25th Division, will now be R.23.a.2045.

2.   ACKNOWLEDGE.

Major. R. A.
Brigade Major, 25th Divisional Arty.

SECRET

ADDENDUM NO. 4 to 25th DIVL.ARTY OPERATION ORDER No. 72.

19th October, 1916.

1. Attack by 74th Inf. Bde will be carried out as follows :-

UNIT.	OBJECTIVE.
13th Cheshires.	R.22.a.3.8. to R.22.b.06 (exclusive).
9th L.N.Lancs.	R.22.b.06 (inclusive) to R.22.b.44 (Railway inclusive)
11th Lancs.Fus:	R.22.b.44 (exclusive) to R.22.a.2.4½ (inclusive).

   Infantry will attack as follows :-

   Each Battalion in three waves.
   First wave - Two companies in line in fighting order, with two Mills bombs per man.
   Second wave - One company in line with five Mills bombs.
   Third wave - One Company in line with five Mills bombs.
   Each man of third wave will have a pick or a shovel tied on his back in the proportion of 1 pick to 3 shovels. If the third wave cannot carry enough tools, a proportion of second wave will also carry them in a similar way.
   Thirty yards distance between waves.

2. The attack must closely follow Artillery barrage as this is essential to success.

3. Directly after assault the following Communication Trenches will be cut by Battalions as follows :-
   13th Cheshires from a suitable point to join into GUNPIT TRENCH.

   9th Loyal North Lancs - R.22.b.1.6.-22.c.8.8. via GUNPIT trench.

   11th Lanc.Fusiliers - from R.22.b.8.2. - 23.a.1.1.

4. ACKNOWLEDGE.

M. Duke
Major, R.A.
Bde Major, 25th Divl.Artillery

Copies to all recipients of 25th Divl.Arty Op.Order No.72.

113th. BRIGADE R. F. A.

25th. DIVISIONAL ARTILLERY

N O V E M B E R   1 9 1 6.

WAR DIARY / INTELLIGENCE SUMMARY

Army Form C. 2118.

113 Brigade RFA
25th Div. Arty

NOVEMBER

Place	Date 1916	Hour	Summary of Events and Information	Remarks and references to Appendices
MOUQUET FARM	Nov 1		Battery positions shelled with 4.2, 5.9 inch during the afternoon	
	3		2/Lieut. T.R.A. DUNCAN joined the Brigade - posted to B.113	
	6		2/Lieuts H.P. MORRISON and H. GRIEVE joined - and posted to C.113 and B.113 respectively.	
	9		'C' Battery heavily shelled from 5 to 5.30 pm with 5.9 and 8 inch. No Casualties. Damage to Equipment	
	10		From 8 pm till 9 to 5' am this morning Battery positions shelled with Gas shells.	
	13		Attack by V Corps N. of the R. ANCRE and by 45, 19 km 39th Divisions II Corps S. of the River. Zero hour 5.45 am. II Corps gained their objective - the HANSA LINE - 'A' Battery shelled during afternoon with 5.9 and 8 inch. One gun damaged & some ammunition blown up.	
	14		2/Lieut. C. H. BLACKBURN joined - posted to A.113.	
	16		Brigade supported the attack of the 18th & Division on DESIRE TRENCH - Zero hour 6.10 am - Objective gained except on the left.	
	18			

Page 2

Army Form C. 2118.

WAR DIARY
or
INTELLIGENCE SUMMARY.
(Erase heading not required.)

Instructions regarding War Diaries and Intelligence Summaries are contained in F.S. Regs., Part II. and the Staff Manual respectively. Title pages will be prepared in manuscript.

Place	Date	Hour	Summary of Events and Information	Remarks and references to Appendices
	21	7 am	Received orders that Brigade will withdraw to wagon lines during the afternoon.	
USNA HILL	22		25 k. D.A. inspected by General JACOBS Comdg. II Corps.	
	23		113 Brigade RFA marches from wagon lines USNA HILL to AMPLIER near DOULLENS -	
	24		Marches to AUBROMETZ	
	25		Marches to MONCHY CAYEUX	
MONCHY	26		Re-organisation of Brigades - (Orders attached)	
CAYEUX	27		Re-organisation completes - Except "C" and "D" Batteries have yet to join.	
			2/Lt. H.R. FILMER joins on the 26 K. - Marches to "C" Battery.	
	28		Marches to RELY. "C" Battery (How:) joins en route	
	29		Marches to STEENBECQUE. 2/Lt. G.W. HASSELL joins - attached to A.113	
	30		Marches to IX Corps Area (near METEREN)	[signature] Lt Col Cmdg 113 Bde RFA

T2134. Wt. W708—776. 500000. 4/15. Sir J.C. & S.

25th. DIVISIONAL ARTILLERY

113th BRIGADE R. F. A.

25th DIVISIONAL ARTILLERY

DECEMBER 1916

113th Brigade RFA. Page 1

WAR DIARY
INTELLIGENCE SUMMARY

Army Form C. 2118.

December
Vol 14

Place: ROMARIN

Date	Hour	Summary of Events and Information	Remarks and references to Appendices
1		The 25th Div will relieve the 74th Div on the line on the 3rd & 4th Dec. 5th U.S./75th BE RFA will relieve the 113th Bde RHA. "A" Battery will relieve "F" Battery. "E" Battery will relieve "T" Battery & "C" Battery will relieve 509 the Howitzer Battery — "D" Battery are relieving D Battery 114th Bde RHA tonight. Battery Commanders went up to Batteries on the morning & will remain.	A.O.(25th DA) No. 96
2		One Officer per Battery went up to reconnoitre.	
3		One section of each Battery relieved a section of the 114th Bde RHA.	
4		Remaining sections of each Battery completed the relief of the 114th Bde by 5 p.m.	
5		Southerly Limits of the Brigade — HQ near LE ROMARIN B.4.b.85. — "A" 113 at PETITE MUNQUE Fm — T.24.a.11 — "B" 113 at T.17.d.42 — "C" 113 at T.23.A.4.9 — D 113 at T.24.d.9.5.	A.O.(36th DA) No. 34
6		The 36th Division are extending their front southwards. The 109th Inf Bde relieving the 75th Inf Bde in the DOUVE SECTOR tonight & tomorrow. The 113th Bde RFA less "C" Battery will be tactically under the command of the 36th Div. Arty.	A.O.(25th DA) No. 87
7		From 10 a.m. this morning the Brigade moved to the 36th DA on their right Group. Nothing to report.	

113 Brigade RFA page 2

WAR DIARY
or
INTELLIGENCE SUMMARY.

(Erase heading not required.)

Army Form C. 2118.

December
Vol XVI

Place	Date	Hour	Summary of Events and Information	Remarks and references to Appendices
	8		Nothing to report	
	9		"	
	10		"	
	11		"	
	12		Observation still very difficult, all guns except for a few rounds both TM from V2d 3.50	
	13		At 11.5 AM this morning an enemy T.M (WILFRED) V.9.b 40.40. opened fire on our trenches. "D" Battery opened & silenced a direct hit by all the fourth round - there was a big explosion with a quantity of smoke & large pieces of timber were flung into the air. Shortly after we learnt that the TM was practically knocked out. U.S.A.A. sent 14 H.E. &	
	14		Operations carried out by the 36th Divisional against PETITE DOUVE extended very successfully. Visibility not good & shortly after the bombardment started became impossible owing to the smoke from the burning brands. Retaliation did not come for about eight minutes & there was very little. It was delivered almost alone by the New Batteries who seemed to have the enemy T.Ms. Battery very well registered - Our fire was very intense & accurate, the enemy trenches being practically destroyed.	A.O. (36th D.A.) No.38.

112/149 Brigade RFA 1917
Army Form C. 2118.
December
Vol. XVI

WAR DIARY
or
INTELLIGENCE SUMMARY.
(Erase heading not required.)

Place	Date	Hour	Summary of Events and Information	Remarks and references to Appendices
			DECEMBER	
	15		Snow had to break up thick layers of ice were frost until the late in the morning reconnaissance	
	16		of front line. Our reconnaissance of the PETITE DOUVE salient	No M.O.D.M
	17		Very little m.g. Battery fired a few rounds on town on PETITE DOUVE to harass enemy	N.3.2
	18		Observation impossible. Hostile artillery active on left of sect. Shoon enemy seen	
	19		A very quiet day. Enemy seemed to be working party on LA PETITE DOUVE	
	20		Detachments of No 25 by O.P. consisting of 1 Officer & 10 N.C.O men Hun S and Battery answered by the Cur-C at 10.30 A.M. R	
			During the day signs of movement on HUNS WALK on front line wood from MESSINES. Enemy aircraft very active – many mach guns seen Battery hostile fired very left out AA guns fired a lot but without success so far as brought our down.	
	21		New heavy TM reported near O.8.3 wads blue "WILFRED" (Bonith) & RS2/mm amm —	
			SM a lot of baffles along HUNS WALK —	
	22		Considerable hostile shelling of our front line by 5.9 & 11.2. Opt R/Russell struck off	
	23		Very quiet all day. Considerable movement reported on HUNS WALK upper line of O.S.H	
	24		Enemy shelled SEAFORTH FARM with 77 amm about 8 AM later about 6 L.150 amm A.W. on NEUVE EGLISE. In full swing our retaliation seemed effective — 2/Lt Hutchinson joined.	

113 Brigade RFA No 4
Army Form C. 2118.
December
Vol. XVI

WAR DIARY / INTELLIGENCE SUMMARY

Place	Date	Hour	Summary of Events and Information	Remarks and references to Appendices
	25		Nothing to report	
	26		Enemy put a number of 4.2 shells into NEUVE EGLISE. Our Gunners silenced him later	
	27		Subsidiary wire laid into S by 54 between 1-3.30 p.m. Otherwise quiet. Spits below to Divisional Hdrs for a long time	
			This Brigade gave out the "retaliation" i.e. shortening going to B.12 central (Map 36 NW) all officers & men from Brigades took it. Gas lines for training except 1 Officer & men per gun & Mess & Signalling per Battery.	AO (25.12.D.1) N3/48
			New positions A/113 at B.6.b.0.7. Four guns the other two to position - B/113 at C.2.a.53. Four guns the other two to position line D/13 at C.1.a.43.	
			The Batteries had under the indirect command of the Right K of Group on & being over next positions but will only be called on for S.O.S. One section of each Battery released - A/113 RFA by C/173 - B/113 by A/172 - D/113 by C/113 - supplied completed by 7.30 p.m. "C" Battery being left in their old position	
	28		Enemy fired about 900.5.9 into GRANDE MUNQUE smashing good shooting. Relief of the Divisional Retired completed by 9.30 p.m.	
	29		The Batteries being broken from no practically there is nothing to report. Programme	

113 Brigade R.F.A. page 1

Army Form C. 2118.

December
Vol XVI

WAR DIARY
or
INTELLIGENCE SUMMARY.
(Erase heading not required.)

Place	Date	Hour	Summary of Events and Information	Remarks and references to Appendices
			DECEMBER	
	29		Training as usual. The Wagon Line called for	
	30		Illustrations. 1st group to new position at B.12 central – Colonel Scourfield D.S.O. took	
	31		over the command of 1st group at 12 noon, while Colonel Townson as near Capt. C. R. H. Hutchinson joined & posted to the command of "A" Battery 2/W.O.R. Muirhead joined & was posted to Headquarters	

Stamford(?)
B.G.

.... Col. R.F.A.
Com'd'g 113th Brigade R.F.A.

S E C R E T.   Copy No. 16

25th DIVL. ARTILLERY ORDER No. 86.

                                                30th November 1916.
Reference Maps 1/20,000
Sheets 28 S.W. & 36 N.W.
----

1.   The 25th Divisional Artillery will relieve the 7th
     Divisional Artillery in the line on the 3rd & 4th
     December.

2.   110th Bde R.F.A. will relieve Right Group (22nd Bde R.F.A.)
     112th Bde   "   "   "   Centre   "   (35th Bde   ")
     113th Bde   "   "   "   Left   "   (14th Bde R.H.A.)
         Batteries of 25th D.A. will relieve Batteries of 7th
     D.A. as shewn in Relief Table (already issued to Brigades)

         One Section of each Battery of 25th D.A. will relieve
     one Section of each Battery of 7th D.A. on 3rd December.
     In addition: 1 gun of C/112 will relieve 1 gun of enfilade
                  section of 58th Bty R.F.A. on 3rd December.
                  1 gun of A/110 will relieve 1 gun of enfilade
                  section of 104th Bty R.F.A. on 3rd December
         The remainder of Brigades & Batteries of 25th D.A. will
     relieve the remainder of Brigades & Batteries of 7th D.A.
     on 4th December.
         Nos 1 & 2 Sections 25th D.A.C. will relieve Nos 1 &
     2 Sections 7th D.A.C. during morning of 3rd December.
         Nos 3 & 4 Sections, 25th D.A.C. will relieve Nos 3 &
     4 Sections 7th D.A.C. during morning of 4th December.
         Details of D.A.C. relief to be arranged by Officers
     Commanding concerned. 25th D.A.C. will be responsible for
     supply of ammunition after 12 noon 4th December.

3.   Incoming Sections of 25th D.A. will be at B.1. central
     at 3 p.m. on 3rd December.
         Two mounted N.C.O's from each Battery of 7th D.A. will
     meet them and conduct them to their Battery positions and
     Wagon Lines.
         Order of march of incoming Sections : 113th Bde.
                                               112th Bde.
                                               110th Bde.

4.   Units of 7th D.A. on relief will march to the billets
     evacuated by 25th D.A.

5.   All movements of 112th & 113th Bdes Westward will be by
     road BRULE GAYE - TROIS ARBRES.
         All movements of 112th & 113th Bdes   n Eastwards will
     be by road DESEULE - TROIS PIPES.

25th D.A. Order No. 86.   Page 2.

Guns will not be exchanged.

25th D.A.C. will take over all ammunition, grenades, S.A.A. etc from 7th D.A.C. at 12 noon 4th December.

Batteries of 25th D.A. will take over all ammunition at gun positions at 12 noon 4th December.

25th D.A. will be responsible for supply of ammunition after 12 noon 4th December.

Receipts will be given for all ammunition taken over.

All Units will forward to H.Q. R.A. not later than 6 p.m. 4th December, a duplicate copy of the receipt for ammunition signed by the Officer Commanding both the incoming and outgoing Unit.

7. 25th D.A. will take over the following as they exist :-
(1) Communications, including all wires to trenches and O.P's and list of Code calls.
(2) All 2nd Army instructions for use of telephones, etc.,
(3) All Orders, circulars, etc.,, which apply to 2nd Army or IXth Corps area.
(4) Trench Maps, Secret Maps, aeroplane photos, fighting map boards, registrations, information as to the front, etc.,
(5) Trench Stores e.g. Soyers Stoves, thigh boots, gas gongs, Strombos horns, dugout equipment and O.P. furniture.
(6) Second Army List of Code Messages.
(7) Second Army Trench Code Book - Instructions for use.
(8) Position Calls.
(9) Instructions for prevention of overhearing.
(10) Second Army Booklet "Instructions for Wind dangerous period etc."
(11) 25th Divn. G.S.14/86 of 7/11/16 -25th Divn.Standing Orders for Gas Discharges.
(12) 25th Divn. G.14/86/1 - Standing orders for Gas Alarms. All 1/10,000 maps of this area.

8. Group & Battery Commanders of 7th D.A. will retain command until the completion of the relief of the whole of their respective Groups & Batteries, when Brigade and Battery Commanders of 25th D.A. will take over command.

9. B.G. R.A. 25th Divn. will assume command at 10 a.m. 5th December.

10. Completion of relief to be reported to H.Q. R.A. 7th Divn. by telephone by the word "MARGARINE".

11. H.Q. R.A. 25th Divn closes at METEREN and opens at BAILLEUL, Rue ST. JACQUES at 10 a.m. 5th December.

12. ACKNOWLEDGE.

M. Duke   Major, R.A.
Bde Major, 25th Divl. Arty.

Copies to :-
O.C. 110th Bde. R.F.A.   7th Div. Arty.
    112th Bde.   "   25th Divn. 'G'
    113th Bde   "   R.A. IXth Corps.
    25th D.A.C.   Heavy Arty IXth Corps.

SECRET.   Copy No. 10a

113 Bde R.F.A.

36TH DIVISIONAL ARTILLERY ORDER No. 34.

1. The 109th Infantry Brigade will be relieved in the SPANBROEK Sector by the 49th Brigade, 16th Division, on the 5th instant and on the same date will relieve the 75th Brigade in the DOUVE Sector.

2. The Tactical Boundaries of the Divisional Front after the move will be :-

   SOUTHERN BOUNDARY.
   U.14.b.8.5 to U.1.d.25.65, along tramline to HYDE PARK CORNER; thence along RED LODGE Road (inclusive to 36th Division) to T.23. Central - G.H.Q. 2nd Line at T.22.a.5.8.
   ONTARIO AVENUE will belong to 25th Division and tramline to 36th Division.

   NORTHERN BOUNDARY.
   DURHAM Road (inclusive to 36th Division) - N.35.d.1.0 - T.4.a. 8.9 - G.H.Q. 2nd Line at N.33.d. 8.4.

3. On completion of Relief the 173rd Brigade R.F.A., will come under the 16th Division for Tactical purposes, and will continue to cover its present front.
   The 113th Brigade R.F.A., 25th Division, will come under the 36th Division, for Tactical purposes, and will continue to cover its present front.

4. The 113th Brigade R.F.A., will become Right Group.
   The 172nd   "   "   "   "   Centre Group.
   The 153rd   "   "   "   "   Left Group.

5. X/36 Trench Mortar Battery will cover the new Right Group Area, and will move from its present positions on the night 5/6th December. This Battery will be under the O.C. 113th Brigade R.F.A., for Tactical purposes.
   The D.T.M.O., 36th Division, will arrange to take over billets vacated by the 2" Trench Mortar Battery of the 25th Division.

6. The Re-Grouping as above will take effect from 10 a.m. 6th December, 1916.

7. A C K N O W L E D G E.

Issued at 5 p.m.
3rd December, 1916.
                                        Major, R.A.,
                           Brigade Major, 36th Divisional Artillery.

Copies to :-

No. 1 to 153rd Bde. R.F.A.,   No. 9 to R.A. IXth Corps.
No. 2 to 172nd   -do-   No. 10 to 25th Divl. Artillery.
No. 3 to 173rd   -do-   No. 11 to 107th Inf. Brigade.
No. 4 to 36th D.A.C.,   No. 12 to 108th Inf. Brigade.
No. 5 to D.T.M.O.,   No. 13 to 109th Inf. Brigade.
No. 6 to 36th Divn. "G",   No. 14 to 36th Div. Signals.
No. 7 to 36th Divn. "Q",   No. 15 to War Diary.
No. 8 to 16th Divl. Arty.   No. 16 to File.

SECRET.   Copy No. 11

25th DIVISIONAL ARTILLERY ORDER No. 87.

                                          4th December, 1916.

1.   The 109th Infantry Brigade, 36th Division, will relieve the
75th Infantry Brigade in the DOUVE Sector on 5th & 6th December, 1916.
     The tactical boundary between 25th Division and 36th Division
will be -
     "The junction of the new trench at U.15.a.0.4. with the
      old front line line trench, to U.14.d.25.65 - along tram
      line to HYDE PARK CORNER - thence along RED LODGE Road
      (inclusive to 36th Division) - to T.23 central -
      thence to G.H.Q. 2nd line at T.22.a.5.8. ONTARIO Ave.
      will be inclusive to 25th Division - INSCROFT Avenue
      and the tramline to 36th Division.

2.   The new Divisional front will be held by 3 Brigades in
the line. The 7th Infantry Brigade will hold as far as
SUFFOLK AVENUE (inclusive); the 75th Infantry Brigade from
SUFFOLK AVENUE (exclusive) to the STRAND (exclusive) - 74th
Infantry Brigade from the STRAND (inclusive) to the left of
the new Divisional front.
     A tracing showing new Brigade areas is attached.

3.   Command of the DOUVE Sector will pass to G.O.C., 36th
Division on completion of relief of 75th Infantry Brigade
by 109th Infantry Brigade.
     Command of Brigade Sectors will pass to G.Os.C.
Brigades from completion of relief.
     Brigade Headquarters will remain as at present.

4.   From the time at which the above relief is completed, the
113th Brigade, less C.Battery, will be tactically under the command
of G.O.C. R.A., 36th Division.
     110th Brigade.R.F.A., less B.Battery (O.C.Lieut.Colonel.Hon.H.
THELLUSON.D.S.O. R.F.A) will cover the 7th Infantry Brigade.
     112th Brigade.R.F.A., with B/110 and C/113 (O.C.Lieut: Colonel
A.B.FORMAN,D.S.O.R.F.A.) will form 2 Sub-Groups.
     112 Right Sub-Group, composed of B/112, B/110, & D/112,
(O.C. Major.C.O.CAREW HUNT.R.F.A.) will cover 75th Infantry Bde.
     112 Left Sub-Group, composed of A/112, C/112, and C/113,
O.C. Captain D.D.H.CAMPBELL.M.C. R.A.) will cover 74th Infantry Bde.

5.   Brigade Commanders of 110th & 112th Brigades will make all
arrangements as to night lines, and Battalion Liaison Officers, with
G.Os.C. Infantry Brigades, as soon as possible, and will report
arrangements made to H.Q.R.A.

6.   Orders as to supply of ammunition, and ammunition returns of
113th Brigade will be issued later.

7.   After the completion of Infantry relief, vide para.4. 112th
Brigade ammunition returns will include returns of B/110 and C/113.

8.   Reports of enemy Artillery, Operation Reports, and Intelligence
reports will be sent to H.Q.R.A. daily by 9.p.m. by
              110th Bde less B.Battery,
              by 112 Right Sub-Group and } through 112 Bde R.F.A.
              by 112 Left Sub-Group   } --------------------

9.   All other administration will be carried out by Brigades as
usual.

10. ACKNOWLEDGE.

                                          Major. R.A.
        Brigad   25th Divl Arty.

105 E Inf. Bde
Neuve Eglise.

SECRET.   Copy No. __1__

36TH DIVISIONAL ARTILLERY ORDER No. 57.

1.   A combined Bombardment of the PETITE DOUVE Salient by Guns, Howitzers and Trench Mortars will take place on Friday, 15th instant, in accordance with attached Table.

2.   Zero time will be at 10.30 a.m. and the Bombardment will last for 30 minutes.
   Watches will be synchronized at 9 a.m.

3.   O.C. Centre Group will arrange details of Bombardment as regards the 2" and Stokes Mortar Batteries.

4.   Co-operation by Machine Guns and Lewis Guns is being arranged.

5.   Any registration required should be carried out as soon as possible.

6.   O.C. Centre Group will inform Brigade Commanders, 108th and 109th Infantry Brigades which Trenches are in the danger zone of the Heavy Trench Mortars.

7.   The 41st Heavy Artillery Group is standing by for Counter-Battery work.

8.   A C K N O W L E D G E.

(signed) C.S.Shanan

Issued at 5 . p.m.
12.12.16.
                     Major, R.A.,
Brigade Major, 36th Divisional Artillery.

Copies:-

No.1 to 113th Bde. R.F.A.,	No.12 to 109th Inf. Bde.
2 to 172nd -do-	13 to O.C.36th Div. Signals.
3 to 153rd -do-	14 to 16th Divl. Arty.
4 to D.T.M.O.,	15 to 25th Divl. Arty.
5 to 36th D.A.C.	16 to No.1.Squadron, R.F.C.,
6 to 36th Divn. "G".	17 to No.2.Kite Balloon Sec:
7 to 36th Division, "Q".,	18 to War Diary.
8 to R.A. IXth Corps.	19 to -do-
9 to H.A. IXth Corps.	20 to File.
10 to 107th Inf. Bde.	21 -do-
11 to 108th Inf. Bde.	

BOMBARDMENT TABLE.

U N I T.	Time.	Task.	No. of rounds.	Remarks.
X,Y & Z, 2" T.M. Batteries.	0.0 - 0.30.	As detailed by O.C. Centre Group.	180 per Battery.	2 rounds a gun a minute.
107th,108th,109th Stokes Batteries.	-do-	-do-	1000 per Battery.	
V/36 H.T.M.Battery. North gun.	-do-	Junction of Trenches U.8.b.4045 & enfilade up Communication Trench running N.E. to U.8.b.7063.	15.	
South Gun.	-do-	U.8.b.0687 & enfilade front line trench.	15.	
Section,9.2" Hows. One Gun.	-do-	U.8.b.2585.	20.	
One Gun.	-do-	Trench U.8.b.4045 - 2585.	20.	
Section, 6" Hows. Both guns.	-do-	Trench U.8.b.4045 - 2585.	50.	
A/113 Bty. (five guns)	-do-	Trench U.8.b. 4045 - 3060.	150 A.X.	
(One gun)	-do-	Enfilade Communication Trench running N.E. from U.8.b. 2585 for a distance of 150 yards.	50 A.	
B/113 Battery.	-do-	Trench U.8.b. 4045 - 3060.	200 A.X.	
D/113 Bty. (Two Guns)	-do-	Communication Trench from U.8.b.1720 - 4045.	} 150 B.X.	
(Two Guns)	-do-	Available for Hostile Trench Mortars as detailed by O.C. Centre Group.	}	

P. T. O.

BOMBARDMENT TABLE (Cont'd).

U N I T.	Time.	Task.	No. of Rounds.	Remarks.
A/172 Bty. (four Guns)	0.0 - 0.30.	U.8.b. 3060 - 2585. Enfilade Communication Trench from U.8.b.4045 running N.E. for a distance of 400 yards.	160 A. X.	
(two Guns)	-do-		80 A.	
B/172 Battery.	-do-	U.8.b. 3060 - 2585.	200 A. X.	
D/172 Bty. (Two Guns)	-do-	Communication Trench from U.8.b.0562 - 2377.		
(Two Guns)	-do-	Available for Hostile Trench Mortars as detailed by O.C. Centre Group.	150 B. X.	

SECRET.   Copy No. 1

36TH DIVISIONAL ARTILLERY ORDER No. 38.

1.   There will be two Artillery concentrations of Fire on the PETITE DOUVE Salient; one at 7 p.m. tonight and the other at 5 a.m. to-morrow morning.

2.   Every Battery that can bring fire to bear on the Salient will fire one round gun fire for each concentration. 18-pdrs. will use shrapnel.

3.   Watches will be carefully synchronized by Group H.Q. with Divisional Artillery H.Q. at 6 p.m.

4.   The Right Group will fire on the front line running N from U.8.a. 95.28.
    The Centre Group will fire on the front line running E from U.8.a. 95.28.
    The Left Group will fire on the Support line trench U.8.b. 40.45 - U.8.b. 75.25.

5.   ACKNOWLEDGE by wire.

                                                                                                                     Major, R.A.,

Issued at 3.30 p.m.
15th December, 1916.   Brigade Major, 36th Divl. Artillery.

Distribution :-

No. 1 to 113th Bde. R.F.A.,   No. 7 to 36th Division "Q".,
    2 to 172nd   -do-   8 to R.A. IXth Corps.
    3 to 153rd   -do-   9 to H.A. IXth Corps.
    4 to 36th D.A.C.,   10 to 107th Inf. Bde.
    5 to D.T.M.O.   11 to 108th Inf. Bde.
    6 to 36th Division, "G".,   12 to 109th Inf. Bde.
                                          Nos.13 & 14 - War Diary.
                                          Nos.15 & 16 - Filed.
                                          No.17 to 16th Divl.Arty.
                                             18 to 25th Divl.Arty.

S E C R E T   Copy No. 1

25th DIVISIONAL ARTILLERY ORDER No. 90.

22nd December, 1916.

1. The 113th Brigade R.F.A. (less C/113) at present covering the 109th Infantry Brigade, 36th Division, will be relieved by 36th Divl. Artillery on nights of 27/28th and 28/29th December, one Section of each Battery being relieved on the first day and the remainder of the battery on the second day. The relief on both days will not be commenced until 4.30 p.m.

O.C. 113th Brigade will arrange details for relief direct with the O.C. relieving Brigade.

2. On relief, batteries of 113th Brigade will be attached for tactical purposes as follows :-

    B. and D. Batteries to Right Group.
    'A' Battery to Centre Group, (which will become Left Group immediately on completion of relief.)

These batteries will proceed direct to the positions already selected for them by Os.C. Right & Left Groups respectively, where they will "rest in action", being available for S.O.S. only.

3. Necessary registration will be carried out under the orders of Group Commanders, as soon as possible from the new positions. When this has been completed 1 Officer, one responsible N.C.O. per Section, 3 telephonists, and 2 men per gun only, will remain at each Battery position, the remainder of the personnel proceeding to the wagon lines.

4. Headquarters 113th Brigade will be at B.12. central.

5. All reliefs and moves will be reported.

6. ACKNOWLEDGE.

                                                                     Major, R.A.
                                             A/g Bde Major, 25th Divl. Arty.

Issued at 4 p.m.

Copies to :-

No.	
1	25th Divn. 'G'.
2.	C.R.A. 36th Divn.
3.	R.A. IXth Corps.
4.	110th Bde R.F.A.
5.	112th Bde. "
6-10.	113th Bde. "
11.	7th Inf. Bde.
12.	74th " "
13.	75th " "
14.	File.
15.	Diary.

A C1a17
B C1b 05.90
C U19c 39
D C1a 53

War Diary
of
113th A.F.A. Bde:
for
February 1917.

Army Form C. 2118.

Vol XVI

Vol/5

WAR DIARY
or
INTELLIGENCE SUMMARY.
(Erase heading not required.)

Instructions regarding War Diaries and Intelligence Summaries are contained in F.S. Regs., Part II. and the Staff Manual respectively. Title pages will be prepared in manuscript.

Place	Date	Hour	Summary of Events and Information	Remarks and references to Appendices
B.12 Central	JANUARY 1917			
	1.		The Batteries not being under one Tactical command here is nothing to report. 'A' and 'C' Batteries are tactically under the command of O.C. Left Group. 'B' and 'D' Batteries under the Right Group - 2/Lieut T.R.A. DUNCAN 'B' Battery attached to W.25 Heavy Trench Mortar Battery.	
	2.		Nothing to report. 2 Lieut D.R. McNIEL transferred from Bde. H.Q. to 'B' Battery.	
	3.		Nothing to report.	
	4.		The following Officers transferred to the 38 R. Div: Arty: with effect from to days date :- 2 Lieuts. W. HORSFIELD - H. GRIEVE - F.V. COUPLAND-SMITH and J.R. FILMER - 2 Lieut B. BEBBINGTON joined on posting from the 38 R. Div: Arty: He is posted to 'C' Battery.	
	5.		Nothing to report.	
	6.		Nothing to report.	
	7.		Nothing to report.	
	8.		Nothing to report.	

Army Form C. 2118.

WAR DIARY
or
INTELLIGENCE SUMMARY.
(Erase heading not required.)

Place	Date	Hour	Summary of Events and Information	Remarks and references to Appendices
	JANUARY 1917			
B.12 Central	9.		At 1.45 PM our artillery and French mortars opened a combined bombardment of the enemy's defences opposite ST. YVES – German front line trench was much knocked about.	
	10.		Orders received re. Re-organization of the 25th Div: Arty: The 113th Brigade RFA is to become an Army Field Artillery Brigade consisting of three 6-gun 18-pdr Batteries, one 6-gun 4.5" Howitzer Battery and a Bde: Amn: Column. To complete the Brigade one 6-gun 18-pdr Battery and a Section of 4.5" Howitzers will be transferred from the 36th Div: Arty: 'C' Battery were split up to-day: Right Section went to D.110 and the Left Section went to D.112. The 113th Army Field Artillery Brigade will, on completion of re-organization, consist of :– HQ 113 Brigade RFA – A/113 – B/113 – B/172 (from 36th D.A.) – D/113 (plus one Section from 36th D.A.) – B.A.C. Re-organization is to be completed by January 31st. Consequent upon the Battery being split up the following transfers in Officers have taken place :– D.110 2/Lieut (Acting Capt.) K.L. IRONSIDE – 2/Lieut R.W.J. GIBBON to D.112. 2/Lieut J.W. HORNE – 2/Lieut B. BEBBINGTON.	

Page 3

Army Form C. 2118.

Vol XVII

WAR DIARY
or
INTELLIGENCE SUMMARY.
(Erase heading not required.)

Place	Date	Hour	Summary of Events and Information	Remarks and references to Appendices
B 12 Central	JANUARY 1917			
	11.		The following transfers took effect from to-days date :- 2 Lieut G.W. HASSALL 'B' to 'D' Battery - 2 Lieut H.P. MORRISON 'B' to Bde. H.Q. - Capt. A. BOOKER from 'A' to 'B' Battery. - Capt. J. SCHOOLING from 'B' to 'A' Battery.	
	12.		Nothing to report.	
	13.		Nothing to report. Hard frost last night -	
	14.		Nothing to report.	
	15.		Re-organization of 25th. Div. Artly: postponed until further orders.	
	16.		Nothing to report.	
	17.		Nothing to report.	
	18.		Nothing to report.	
	19.		About 12 NOON Six 8" Howitzer (?) shells fell near 'B' Battery position at C 2 a 40.30 - Extract from "London Gazette" dated 16.1.17 Lieut. to be Captain. C.R.M. HUTCHISON M.C. with effect from 20.12.16	
	20.		Nothing to report	
	21.		— ditto —	
	22.		At 1.15 PM the enemy opened a bombardment along the whole Divisional front. The enemy raided our trenches at U 22 c and U 15 d - One man in 'B' Battery killed by a premature from a Battery in rear.	

Page 4.
Army Form C. 2118.
Vol XVII

WAR DIARY
or
INTELLIGENCE SUMMARY.
(Erase heading not required.)

Place	Date	Hour	Summary of Events and Information	Remarks and references to Appendices
			JANUARY. 1917	
B.M. Central	23.		Nothing to report. Lieut F.F. MEADOWS 'A' Battery transferred to 'B' Battery A.A. Group.	
	24.		Lieut Colonel F.F. LAMBARDE having this day proceeded on leave Major C.R.M. HUTCHISON assumes command of the Brigade.	
	25.		Orders received that Bde. HQ. 'A' and 'B' Batteries must hold themselves in readiness to move at short notice, in the event of the Corps on our Right and Left or the VIII K. Corps requiring assistance.	
	26.		Nothing to report	
	27.		Nothing to report	
	28.		Nothing to report	
	29.		Nothing to report.	
	30.		— ditto —	
	31.		— ditto —	

C.R.M. Hutchison
Maj. R.F.A.

Col. R.F.A
Comdg 113th Brigade R.F.A.

Army Form C. 2118.

113th Army
Brigade RFA
Vol 16

WAR DIARY
or
INTELLIGENCE SUMMARY

(Erase heading not required.)

Instructions regarding War Diaries and Intelligence Summaries are contained in F.S. Regs., Part II. and the Staff Manual respectively. Title Pages will be prepared in manuscript.

Place	Date	Hour	Summary of Events and Information	Remarks and references to Appendices
B.H.Q. Meteren			February	
	1		2/Lt G.W. Marsden reported at 25th Divisional Signalling School at METEREN for nine months Signalling Course.	
	2		About 5.30 p.m. the enemy started a heavy bombardment of our front & support line from C.4.a. to U.28.a. — All quiet by 7.30 p.m. — Nothing to report. O.C. "A" Battery reconnoitered position for two guns near Steple Rode Corner. Position required for wire cutting at "the Louvre" Farm at A Battery Wagon Line broken down.	
	3		Nothing to report.	
	4		St Col. Saumarde & Major Osborne returned from leave.	
	5		Nothing to report.	
	6		"	
	7			
	8			
	9		Capt Schooling to No 10 Ordnance Depot AUDRICQ.	
	10		Nothing to report.	
	11		Order issued to start Reorganisation. B.A.C. to be formed at	

Army Form C. 2118.

WAR DIARY
or
INTELLIGENCE SUMMARY
(Erase heading not required.)

Instructions regarding War Diaries and Intelligence Summaries are contained in F. S. Regs., Part II. and the Staff Manual respectively. Title Pages will be prepared in manuscript.

Place	Date	Hour	Summary of Events and Information	Remarks and references to Appendices
B 10 Central			February -	
	11		DAGSHAI LINES on the 12th	
			Lieut J.B. Philpin joined the Brigade & was posted to Y/25 Trench Mortar Battery	
	12		Personnel moved etc. from D/113 Transferred to B.A.C. Capt. Elliot posted to B.A.C. from 25th D.A.C. 2/Lt Blackburn attached to B.A.C. from A/113 -	
	13		Formation of B.A.C. continued	
	14		113th BDE R.F.A. became 113th Army Bde T.F.A.	
	15		Nothing to report.	
	16			
	17			
	18		Captain Schooling returned -	
	19		Captain Schooling transferred from "A" Battery to command of the B.A.C. 2/Lt S.W. Dais posted to B.A.C. on first commission. Capt. Elliot attached to A/113.	
	20		Nothing to report	
	21		Final orders received to complete reorganization by 22nd Guns withdrawn from the line. 31st/DA	
	22		Brigade moved into new area — C/113 took B/172 - & one section of D/113	WSC 784/33

2449 Wt. W14957/M90 750,000 1/16 J.B.C. & A. Forms/C.2118/12.

WAR DIARY
or
INTELLIGENCE SUMMARY

(Erase heading not required.)

Army Form C. 2118.

Place	Date	Hour	Summary of Events and Information	Remarks and references to Appendices
NEUVE EGLISE	22		Late C/172 joined up at Wagon Lines. Details from new Wagon Lines — Horses — H.Q T.14 b 90 — Horses T 20 a 20. A/113 S.5 b 43. B/113 M 34 d 28. C/113 S5 b 36. D/113 T 27 c 42. BAC S.5 b 96. All units reported arrived, & details joined up by 6 p.m. — Sent J.H.S. Pownall NCO for Overseas Gunnery Course. Lieut. J. Edwards from late C/172 to B.A.C. 2/Lt. G.O. Stead from late C/172 to B.A.C.	Map ref. 28 S.W. 1/20,000
	23		Nothing to report.	
	24		"	
	25		"	
	26		"	
	27		"	
	28		"	

Hawkridge Major
CmdG 113 Bde RFA

www.ingramcontent.com/pod-product-compliance
Lightning Source LLC
Chambersburg PA
CBHW081408160426
43193CB00013B/2133